RADIANT

Priscilla Shirer

RADIANT

His light, your life

FOR TEEN GIRLS AND YOUNG WOMEN

B&H
PUBLISHING
NASHVILLE, TENNESSEE

Published by B&H Publishing Group
Nashville, Tennessee

Dewey Decimal Classification: 248.83
Subject Heading: SELF-REALIZATION / GIRLS / TEENAGERS

For Wynter

Contents

Those who look to him are

RADIANT

their faces are never covered
with shame.

PSALM 34:5 NIV

I am who God says I am.
I can do what God says I can do.
I can become exactly what God says I can become.

I'm not defined by my feelings, my weaknesses,
or my inclinations, and I will not devalue what
He has made me to be by comparing it to what
seems better and brighter in someone else.

I am coming out of the lies.
I am coming into the light.

HELLO, MY NAME IS...

I once gave myself a new name.

And, no, I'm not joking.

After attending a private Christian school from kindergarten through eighth grade, I transferred to a nearby public school for my freshman year, where almost none of the other students or any of the teachers knew me. And at the last minute, I decided it would be a fun experiment to change my name.

So I did.

I decided not to be "Priscilla" anymore.

Somehow, it made perfect sense in my teenage mind to change my name to something else—something cooler, I thought, something quirkier—a clever nickname I decided I wanted to be called by. (I'll spare you the detail of telling you what it is. It would take a whole other chapter to explain what could possibly have seemed intriguing about it.)

I can still see my friend Nicole from the youth group at church going around that first day, helping introduce me to people. We'd pass other kids in the hallway, and she'd say to them, "Hey, y'all, this is Pri—I mean, uh," pausing to shoot me an inquisitive squint, as if to say, *Girl, are we really going through with this?*

Yes, I was.

And, yes, I did.

And guess what? It worked! By the time I graduated, not one teacher, not one student, not one coach or member of the school administration referred to me by any other name than the one I'd handpicked for myself. Even my sports uniforms and letterman's jacket were monogrammed with it. I'd successfully renamed myself. In fact, to this day, if someone ever passes me around town or addresses me on social media by that name, I know it's someone I went to high school with.

Now, my parents didn't seem to mind it too much back then—my informal, impromptu decision to be called by another name. I think they saw it as nothing more than a teenage girl thing. A phase. No big deal. But as my senior year began winding down, my mother, who'd mostly held her tongue on how she felt about it, decided she needed to speak up. With an official graduation ceremony approaching in the near future, where she'd be forced to sit and watch me cap my high school career to the sound of a different name from the one she'd given me at birth, she decided she'd kept her opinion to herself long enough. She cornered me in the house one day and, with a "this is your mama speaking" directness to her voice, said: *"Priscilla . . . !"*

Followed by something like this . . .

> *When I see you walk across that stage at graduation, I'd better not hear or see your little nickname anywhere in the vicinity of your diploma. Because no matter how many people call you that, it is not your name. The only two people who have the right to give you your name are your dad and I. And your name is the one we gave you on the day you were born.*

Point made. Not so much loud as *clear*. At the time, I didn't realize the important life lesson this harmless high school experience would teach me. But I see it now. This was about more than just a nickname. It was about identity. No one else besides the One who made you has the right to give you your *true* name. Not even *you* have the right to give yourself that name, to redefine who you are. Any label that is different from the one your heavenly Father gave you is flat-out false.

Even if, like me, you choose a new name, a new identity doesn't come with it. Only the One who gave you life can give you your identity.

"I have called you by your name," God said to His people. "You are mine" (Isaiah 43:1). You are "precious in my sight and honored, and I love you . . . everyone who bears my name and is created for my glory. I have formed them; indeed, I have made them" (vv. 4, 7).

He has made us. And He has named us.

And His name for you, little sister, is your real and only name. Your identity and significance come from Him. Not what others have said (or haven't said, no matter how much you've wished they would). Not the mistakes you've made (or haven't made, which may have led you to think too highly of yourself and feel a bit judgmental of others). Not the secret desires you harbor, the weaknesses you've indulged, the abuses you've endured, or even the successes you've achieved.

No, your Father's name for you—the core value He has placed in you—is the one that eclipses all others and gives you true significance no one can take away.

But if you're like most people, you've given yourself some names and labels over the years that have gradually become part of how you think about yourself. They're part of the perspective through which you view your life and your future. Maybe, unlike how I did it in high school, you don't go around calling yourself by that name out loud, in public, where everyone can hear you. But in the privacy of your own heart, when no one's around to know any better, you deride yourself with distorted summary statements that contain false readings on *who you are,* because of what you've done, or how you feel, or experiences you've had.

Or maybe you've simply begun answering to some of the names other people have had the nerve to hang on you. Hurtful nicknames. Pointed jabs of disrespect and jealousy and ugliness. You hear them; you repeat them; you absorb them; you rehearse them. But if you don't reject them, they mar your sense of identity like chewing gum on the bottom of your shoe. Hard to get off without leaving a smudge.

It's also possible that the name someone calls you may not be particularly hurtful, but it is equally damaging because it swings to the other extreme, coddling your pride and indulging your self-centeredness. I have a friend whose parents consistently referred to her as their "perfect princess" when she was growing up—an endearing, harmless nickname, but one that became problematic when they treated her as royalty to match the name. They gratified every whim, caved to every tantrum, and catered to her every wish. She was the spoiled center of the family's universe and became accustomed to receiving every single drop of attention.

Of course, all this felt good to her. None of it was bad or hurtful or hard to deal with. But the whole "princess" thing failed to help balance her sense of humility and compassion toward others. She grew up with an air of pride, superiority, and entitlement that became a major hang-up into adulthood. She lost friends, she cost herself opportunities, and she struggled to find intimacy in her relationship with God—all because she'd been put on a pedestal and figured it was hers to keep forever, that everyone else should treat her as if she belonged there too. But over time, she found out the hard way that God didn't exist to serve her. She was His beloved child, yes, but she'd been re-created in Christ Jesus to serve *Him*. She wasn't perfect. But He was, and she needed Him. She had to climb down from that pedestal, learn about God's real purposes for her life, and realize He wasn't there to grant her every selfish desire. Her whole life changed when she found out her name.

Names matter.

Your name matters.

The true name given by the One who created you.

Even when . . .

ever-changing standards of beauty
whisper, "You're **UGLY***";*

a teacher who embarrasses you, or a
camp counselor who overlooks you,
makes you feel **WORTHLESS;**

the clique that won't accept you or people
who refuse to include you communicate
that you're **UNWANTED;**

people who laugh at you instead of
affirming and celebrating you convince
you that you're **UNLOVED;**

that guy who won't look at you, or brushes
you aside instead of treasuring you, makes
you see yourself as **REJECTED;**

the social media feed that haunts you,
displaying the lives of more popular,

seemingly more perfect people than you, makes you feel even more **INVISIBLE;**

the tears you cry, the hurts you nurse, the wounds you bear deep inside your heart, scream to you that you're **BROKEN;**

the secret habit you indulge, again and again, hopeless that you can ever change, continually leaves you feeling **BOUND;**

the coach who keeps nitpicking you, convincing you that you'll never measure up, makes you feel **INADEQUATE;**

the circumstances surrounding your birth or, worse, the people who bring it up again to hurt you at your most vulnerable moments, tell you that you're a **MISTAKE;**

that horrible thing you did, that terrible sin you committed, sneers at you, shames you, and says you're **UNFORGIVABLE;**

the lust you willingly gave in to, or the innocence that evil stole from you, keeps whispering that you are **IMPURE.**

"I'm **STUPID.***"*

"I'm **FORGOTTEN.***"*

"I'm **DIRTY.***"*

"I'm a **TOTAL FAILURE.***"*

Do any of these names sound familiar? Do they echo in your mind? In your heart? In the sound of your own voice? Or maybe in the tone of someone else's—someone who should have built you up but chose instead to tear you down?

No matter how you hear them and why you may have chosen to believe them, none of these lies is your true name or identity. Not even one of them. Why? *Because this is not what your Father calls you.* And you are who He says you are.

Point-blank. Period.

That's why I've purposely and intentionally called this book *Radiant,* because "those who look to him are radiant; their faces are never covered with shame" (Psalm 34:5 NIV). That's who you are. And the more you see *why* you're radiant, the more this truth will help you. When times are tough, when life disappoints, when struggles abound, when your friends fail, when you question your own significance and purpose—in all these situations and more, you are still exactly who God says you are, and you can accomplish everything He says you can.

God's radiance shines through you, through the uniqueness of you. Everything about the way He's created you, He did it with the purpose of making you a prism for His light. You're like an intricately designed stained glass window made of beautiful and unique details, distinct in certain ways from all others. And *through* you, through the carefully constructed window of your life's uniqueness and experiences (even the hard ones), He wants to show Himself to the world.

So all the things that come together to make you a unique package of combinations—your gender as a woman, your race and culture, the way your body is made, the way your favorite ideas and interests intersect, the good and bad experiences you've had, even the weaknesses you carry around inside you— God planned or allowed all these things for a reason. And the reason is because you provide Him a one-of-a-kind outlet for showing His grace and greatness to everyone who sees you.

So I'm calling you to be vigilant and proactive—to be careful and on your guard—or else you'll begin to define yourself differently. You'll label yourself by a flawed narrative. Then your attitudes and behavior will start to reflect it. You'll start living down to your false names instead of rising up into the radiance of who you really are.

It's time to tune in to a different station, one that rings with truth. You need to block out the lies that keep trying to undermine your true stature as a daughter of the King, because your value in Him will never change even when your circumstances do. Knowing and really believing your God-given identity will save you from searching for significance in all the wrong people, positions, and possessions. None of these things can give you worth or lasting value. Only your Father can do that.

Change the narrative. Reprogram your perspective. Rehearse and internalize truth as your weapon against the lies that are so easy to come by. The names that God in His Word has given and ascribed to you are the names you need to answer to and accept as your own.

UGLY?

"Listen, daughter, pay attention and consider . . . and the king will desire your beauty." (PSALM 45:10–11)

WORTHLESS?

"He will redeem them . . . for their lives are precious in his sight." (PSALM 72:14)

UNWANTED?

Behold what manner of love the Father has bestowed on us, that we should be called children of God!" (1 JOHN 3:1 NIV)

REJECTED?

"You did not choose me, but I chose you." (JOHN 15:16)

INVISIBLE?

"Where can I go to escape your Spirit? Where can I flee from your presence? . . . Even [at the ends of the earth] your hand will lead me; your right hand will hold on to me." (PSALM 139:7, 10)

BROKEN?

"May the God of peace Himself sanctify you through and through [that is, separate you from profane and vulgar things, make you pure and whole and undamaged— consecrated to Him—set apart for His purpose]." (1 THESSALONIANS 5:23 AMP)

INADEQUATE?

"I am able to do all things through him who strengthens me." (PHILIPPIANS 4:13)

HOPELESS?

"Whatever was written in the past was written for our instruction, so that we may have hope." (ROMANS 15:4)

UNFORGIVABLE?

"I am writing to you, little children, since your sins have been forgiven on account of his name." (1 JOHN 2:12)

HORRIBLE? IMPURE?
A MISTAKE? A FAILURE?

"I have been remarkably and wondrously made." (PSALM 139:14)

You are chosen, accepted, valuable, desired.

This. Is. Who. You. Are.

Stop calling yourself a name that's not even yours—never has been; never will be. Today is the day to answer to your Father.

Listen. Do you hear Him calling?

Daughter, you are Mine.

PART ONE

LET THERE BE LIGHT

Read This

It was you who created my inward parts; you knit me together in my mother's womb. I will praise you because I have been remarkably and wondrously made. Your works are wondrous, and I know this very well. (PSALM 139:13-14)

Say This

I am divinely designed, handcrafted by God inside and out, created to reflect His light to people around me. I am made in His image. This means the things that make me different are not mistakes or liabilities. They are the outworking of His creative genius. They make me exactly who He meant me to be—"remarkably and wondrously made." A flat-out radiant miracle.

Believe This

God created man in his own image; he created him in the image of God; he created them male and female. . . . God saw all that he had made, and it was very good indeed. (GENESIS 1:27, 31)

2

WHAT A WONDER

One year at Christmas, my siblings and I got a Big Wheel. Have you heard of it? A Big Wheel is a mostly plastic, brightly colored, low-slung take on a tricycle, and to the under-ten crowd of my day—like my brothers and sister and me—it was a prized possession.

We tore off the wrapping paper from the enormous cardboard box and opened it with an excited frenzy. Because despite the fact that it was only six o'clock in the morning, we couldn't wait to start riding it up and down the driveway. Except . . . we couldn't . . . because the Big Wheel underneath the tree on that bright Christmas morning hadn't come as a fully formed toy ready to roll. For the moment, it was just a big box with pieces of unassembled Big Wheel inside of it, which we begged our dad to hurry up and put together.

And he did—or at least he tried—a task we four kids didn't make any easier on him by pelting him every few minutes with our impatience. He grew frustrated and fatigued as he labored at fitting the oddly shaped pieces together.

After about an hour had gone by, our mom started to worry

this project might keep him working well into the afternoon. So she strode into the garage, where my poor daddy was still feverishly trying to make connections. She carefully stepped around all the various parts of Big Wheel strewn across the floor, drew up close to him, placed a tender hand on his shoulder, and uttered the one question that helped get things moving in the right direction: "Honey, why don't you read the instructions?"

Good idea, Mom . . . because the manufacturer is the one who knows best how things are supposed to fit together. The manufacturer is able to accurately identify all the pieces and tie them into place, into a completed whole. To top it off, the manufacturer even provides a manual to read so we can know how to handle his creation the way he intended.

I think you know what I'm getting at. The God who made you has given you the Bible, His Word, not only so you can understand all the individual pieces of your identity that make you unique and special, but also to show you how to see them as an intact, purposeful unit. How to like what you see when you put it all together. How to get out there and ride, take this show on the road, actually *live* the life He's imagined for you and made possible for you.

So, whether you're a black girl, white girl, brown girl, or any color girl in between—tall girl, short girl, athletic girl, academic girl—blonde girl, redhead girl, or brunette girl, suburban girl or inner-city girl, poor girl or rich girl—all of us girls, all of us women, need our Manufacturer's instructions for perspective and guidance. Life will be really frustrating without them.

And I can't think of any better insight from the Manual to start out with than this . . .

> *It was you who created my inward parts; you*
> *knit me together in my mother's womb. I will*

14

praise you because I have been remarkably and
wondrously made. Your works are wondrous,
and I know this very well. (PSALM 139:13–14)

Created . . . knit together . . . remarkably . . . wondrously. These are such good words, in fact, that I think I'll repeat them for you in a Bible paraphrase called *The Message,* just to make sure they land on you at every level of impact.

Oh yes, you shaped me first inside, then
out; you formed me in my mother's womb. I
thank you, High God—you're breathtaking!
Body and soul, I am marvelously made! I
worship in adoration—what a creation!

These verses, these words from your Manufacturer, tell you some things you need to know about yourself by first telling you some things you need to know about Him.

He made you. On purpose. By design.
He put you together in your mother's body.
He has an intimate, involved knowledge of you.
He possesses a deep interest and concern for you.
He didn't create you by chance or by accident.
He made you with your whole life in mind.
Wonderful God created a wonderful you.

Now, to tell you the truth, it's a wonder He made any of us at all. That's part of what's so *wonderful* about the fact that He created us . . . because He sure didn't need to. It's not like He was missing something from His life before we came along. He is God. He's always been God. He is fully complete within Himself. He made you—get this!—*because He wanted you.*

But He further shows His love for you in the meticulous, miraculous way He designed you, which when you really consider it, when you really believe it, ought to fill you with a deep, internal wonder. More likely, though, if you tend to see yourself the way a lot of us do, you overlook and downgrade your design on a regular basis. Boring. Mundane. Lacking. Insufficient. We tend to highlight the parts we don't like—the parts we've been outright told or passively made to feel are negatives, like our loud voice or our introverted nature, our narrow nose or our wide feet, our disinterest in sports or our clumsiness in general. God's intentionality behind our creation, however, should shake us out of these doldrums and lift our chins to the possibilities of our potential.

You were created *intentionally* and with painstaking attention to detail.

I wish this revelation about being "wondrously made" had occurred to me back in high school. I wish I'd understood and trusted God more, in terms of the individual person He divinely created me to be. Like how He intended for me to have . . .

- this thick, curly, unruly hair;
- a face punctuated by a slightly oversized nose, for which I was ruthlessly teased in school;
- a gregarious personality, sharing space with a slightly fierce rebellious streak;
- a tendency to talk too much and listen too little;
- a weakness in math (complete disinterest, really), as well as in every single thing related to science.

I think if I'd put Psalm 139 and Priscilla side by side and tried to square myself up against the truth of what God said about me, I'd have been able to relax into myself more. I would've been able to submit my entire body to Him and see it as an instrument that reflected His light to others.

I think I would've better appreciated my distinct quirks and inclinations instead of trying to conform them or hide them or change them into something more applauded and accepted.

I think I would've realized that my distinctions—when surrendered to Him—were designed to be the very things that would roll out the red carpet for me to walk into my calling and operate in my destiny. I needed to look like *this,* and think like *this,* and relate to others like *this* to fulfill the purpose for which I was created.

Not only that, I think I would've realized that my weaknesses didn't make me bad or of lesser value. They just offered an opportunity for God to demonstrate His strength through me in a unique way, shining the radiance of His light through the prism of my life. Yeah, He'd *planned* these frailties and quirks—the things that didn't come easily for me—as opportunities for Him to uniquely use me. Every nuance of my being was meant to show me what He could do if I'd start to see everything He'd made in me as being purposeful.

As being wonderful. Radiantly wonderful.

His light in my life.

. .   .   .
.   .

Not too long ago, I sat on one of the hard, wooden pews in my grandfather's church, a dignified but aging little building in Baltimore's inner city. Barely a dozen members had gathered that day, same as they do every Sunday—to worship, to see each other, to hear my ninety-year-old grandfather preach.

It's not a fancy place. A box fan cools it in the summer, just as a heavy, hot-to-the-touch radiator warms it through the Maryland winter. Some of the keys on the piano, which sits off to one side, are noticeably out of tune, punctuated by singing voices that are rich in faith and the experiences of life.

I was absorbing this nostalgic scene, same as I'd done during so many trips there in my childhood, and that's when I noticed something. A gleaming patch of multicolored light suddenly caught the corner of my eye, painting itself on part of the row where I was seated. Its movements were imperceptible, like the hands of an old analog clock. Yet after each few minutes, the light had inched itself a bit nearer to me, occupying a slightly different place, lengthening and shifting, shimmering, glistening . . .

Beautiful.

Turning my head to see where the light had come from, I noticed the stained glass windows built into the otherwise plain brown paneled walls of my granddaddy's church. The sun shining through had illuminated them into full bloom. So vibrant. The uniqueness of each window, as it caught the rays of outdoor light, created a dazzling kaleidoscope effect of color. Rich and deep. Transparent glory. Each reflection was like an explosion of beauty. Unique and alive.

Soon, one of those shafts of light was glistening on a portion of my sleeve. After a while, it had even worked its way across my body and into my lap. I could move my hand in and out of it, the same way I'd done as a child, marveling at how its warmth and radiance contoured around my skin in such a vivid and distinct manner. Each window a unique display, an individual reflection of the light.

Stained glass windows, like the ones you see in ornate churches and cathedrals, or even like the less elaborate ones I saw that morning, are remarkable for at least two reasons.

First is their *uniqueness*. Windows like these are not made casually, mindlessly. A gifted artisan selects various shards and shapes of glass and then fashions them into precise positions. Every curve, every corner, every shade, every nuance and detail, is intentionally chosen and cemented into place. No part of it—not even the smallest, least noticeable piece—is a throwaway. Nothing is unnecessary. The designer meticulously fits them all together, bringing to life the vision he saw in his mind before he even began creating his art. His goal is to craft something unique that will beautifully reflect the light.

Light, then, is the second thing to notice about these windows. The craftsman knows what he wants the stained glass to look like when the light shines through it—how it will be seen by others, how it will be received by those who stand in its glow and admire it. Being a prism for the light is the window's real function, and reflecting the light well is its highest achievement. Because if not for the light, that same window, created in the same way, might be pretty, but it wouldn't be purposeful. It would produce only darkness. On its own, it has no ability to transmit the radiance it was created to emit.

Like a beautifully created, intentionally crafted stained glass window, you have been designed by a master Artisan with distinction in mind. You're the only one He chose to make exactly as He created you—in your own shape and coloring, with your own individuality, personality, and background. *Your uniqueness.* He made you this way not only so you could be special, but because He'd already thought ahead about how best He could accomplish His ultimate goal through you. To reflect the light. *His light.*

The light is what fires the masterpiece of your unique being to life.

His radiant light is what fires you to life.

"You know me inside and out," the Bible says. "You know every bone in my body; you know exactly how I was made, bit by bit, how I was sculpted from nothing into something" (Psalm 139:15 MSG).

Hear me clearly: God put you together in a specific fashion. He made you with precision. He made you with in-depth planning. He made you with an incredible amount of personal involvement. "Like an open book, you watched me grow from conception to birth; all the stages of my life were spread out before you, the days of my life all prepared before I'd even lived one day" (v. 16 MSG).

You—your physical attributes (*who you are* on the outside) . . .

You—your internal uniqueness (*who you are* on the inside) . . .

You—your life circumstances (*who you are* in time and space) . . .

This person—you—did not just happen at random, as if any old thing would do. You are not a mistake or an afterthought. Your individual strengths and weaknesses, your individual quirks and abilities, your individual past and experiences—it's all unique, and it's all on purpose.

> *How can what is made say about its maker,*
> *"He didn't make me"? How can what is formed*
> *say about the one who formed it, "He doesn't*
> *understand what he's doing"?* (ISAIAH 29:16)

He knew exactly what He was doing when He made *every-thing* about you, even the parts you've been told are not beautiful, important, or valuable—unacceptable—even the parts you've been told won't be helpful to your future or will keep you from being able to excel. He made you with this core distinctiveness for a specific purpose that can only be accom-plished through your unique mixture of physicality and per-sonality, when you yield them to Him. He did it so others could see, through the reflection of your life, something special about *who God is*, "being understood through what he has made" (Romans 1:20). Just as the reflected light of the sun causes the nighttime moon to be a "faithful witness in the sky" (Psalm 89:37), the reflected light of God through the window of your life makes you a testimony of His love, His grace, His goodness, His power, His creative genius, and more.

You are you, but you are His. Everything about you.

Even the parts you may not much like or prefer.

They're more wonderful than you know.

3

A HAIR STORY
(WHAT'S YOUR STORY?)

My whole life, I have wrestled or relished (depending on my mood that day) this thick wad of naturally curly goodness on top of my head.

Throughout my childhood my mom parted my hair straight down the center, with two broad, lopsided braids hanging down, one on each side. But during my teen years I embarked on the exciting and complicated process of permanently straightening my hair, seeking to give it more of that layered, longer, bouncier effect, which was by far the most popular way of wearing it for African American women in the 1990s.

I was a high school cheerleader, one of only two black girls on the team in our gigantic high school, where being able to fit my hair into a long, loose ponytail with an enormous red-and-blue bow around it was a squad *requirement*—despite the fact that my hair didn't do this on its own. It took hours of salon treatment, and money, and all kinds of special things to buy and use to fit that mold. Worse, though, it involved introducing harsh chemicals into my hair and scalp that literally *burned* me if those products were applied for even a moment longer than prescribed. Over time, this process of relaxing my hair made it thin and brittle, weak and broken.

But also, *straight*.

And straight—and sameness—were more important to me than anything.

For curly-haired girls, the pressure to conform in this area has historically been quite high, and many of us have submitted ourselves to costly, caustic regimens of hairstyling, simply because we haven't liked (or haven't known how to manage) the hair we were born with.

But in my early twenties, I started to get concerned—enough that I scheduled an appointment with my doctor to ask her a few questions about some issues I was having. I'd started to notice I was developing big patches of burned-off stubble on my head where hair used to be. The decision I'd made as a teenager to straighten my natural hair had resulted in making it completely unhealthy. I'd been hurting myself trying to look like someone I wasn't. But here's the thing: In my youth, I didn't care! I just wanted my hair to be straight, and I wanted to fit in—*more than* I wanted to maintain my own health.

Still, I was certain these problems I'd been experiencing could easily be rectified. I stepped into my sweet doctor's office with a hopeful outlook. Confident but . . . okay, still pretty edgy because . . . *My hair! I'm losing my hair! Arghhh!*

My appointment went a little something like this:

ME (in dramatic fits of hysteria): *Dr. Diane, help me! My hair is thinning and my scalp is irritated. Can you prescribe something to fix it, please? Today?*

DR. DIANE (calmly, delicately fingering through my scalp and hair): *Other than washing and combing it, what are you doing to your hair regularly?*

ME (a single tear running down my cheek, violins playing in the background): *I get a relaxer to straighten it every six weeks.*

DR. DIANE (without pause): *I'm pretty sure those chemicals are damaging your hair. You'll need to stop doing it for at least the next six months, or this problem is going to get much, much worse.*

Silence.

Blank staring.

Crickets chirping.

She was so casual when she said it. So matter-of-fact . . . as if she hadn't just given me a directive that would end my social life as I knew it. Did she realize what she was saying? Did she not know that if I made this change she was ordering, my hair would return to being a bushy, gravity-defying afro? No way on God's green earth could this middle-aged white doctor have any idea how unbelievably impossible and unfathomable the concept she was suggesting would be for a woman of color to hear and internalize. Not getting a relaxer wasn't something we did back then. It's just wasn't. It would mean just—*gasp!*—letting our hair go natural.

It was simply unheard-of, at the time. For most of us back then, once you crossed the threshold of womanhood where your mother allowed you to finally apply a permanent straightener to your hair, it was sort of a rite of passage from which you never returned . . . not willingly anyway. You were committed. For life. And whatever issues came along with the commitment, you just worked through them. Or ignored them. It was a marriage. And divorce was not an option.

For better or worse.

In sickness and health.

Till death do us part.

Amen.

Now, you may not be familiar with hair issues like this. Possibly you don't have a "hair story." But I'm certain you have a story of your own. Most young women have one—a love-hate relationship with one or any number of physical attributes that you've been made to feel uncomfortable about. Your complexion or your jeans size. Your measurements or your eyebrows. For me, it was my hair. So when I left the doctor's office that day, I had no intention of obeying her orders. I mean, I couldn't, right? I was stubborn and unmoved.

But something happened to me on that drive home . . . something I can't quite explain, except to say that the Holy Spirit started digging past the hair on my head, straight down into my heart. Whether or not I straightened my hair wasn't an issue of right and wrong. That's merely aesthetics. But *why* was I more interested in making my hair straight than making it healthy? That was the critical issue. For me, it became a question of *why*.

- *Why was I doing this?*
- *Who was I trying to please?*
- *What was this decision costing me?*
- *Where was this desire truly coming from?*
- *Why was it so important to me that I fit in?*
- *Why was I willing to sacrifice my health to look a certain way?*
- *And what did all my hesitation and resistance say about how my sense of value and worth was wrapped up in the appearance of my hair? Why was I so scared to . . . just . . . be . . . me?*

The answers to these questions shined the spotlight on a deep-seated, misplaced sense of value, exposing how much weight I'd illegitimately placed on the approval and acceptance of others. It had been so important for me to meet a standard of beauty—first in my school, then later as a young adult in society—that I was now willing to ignore doctor's orders and sacrifice myself to obtain it.

Was I really going to forgo my own health to achieve sameness? Was I so insecure that I needed to have straight hair to feel acceptable?

By the time I got home, tears were falling, my heart had grown tender, and my mind was changed. I wanted to take care of myself.

I would never chemically straighten my hair again.

And I haven't.

It was the year 2000 when I made the unpopular decision (*extremely* unpopular at the time) to stop using chemicals on my hair and let it grow back in its original state, the wondrous way God made it.

You'd be amazed if I told you how many people tried to convince me I was out of my mind for doing this, despite the health issues I was facing. But I did it anyway. (I guess that rebellious streak was good for something after all.) And it's proved to be one of the best personal decisions I've ever made in my life.

In the months and years that followed, my hair began to heal. Learning to appreciate and take care of my new, natural hair took time, diligence, and patience, for sure. But I found to my surprise that I grew a head of thick, curly hair—more spectacular and unique than anything I could have imagined for myself. I explored and experimented, finding friends and influencers who were knowledgeable enough to help me and were also encouraging enough to support me. It took quite a village, I discovered, to learn how to be myself, which sounds like an odd thing to say. But when you've lived so long as a shadow of yourself, it takes help to be introduced to your authentic self again.

Twenty years later, the choice to accept, celebrate, and enjoy my natural hair is one I've never regretted. I only wish I'd made it sooner.

Because let me tell you what happened when I did. Not only did it give me the courage to reflect my individuality in other areas of my life, but the ripple effect on the lives of other girls and women was staggering . . . and nearly immediate. In the years that directly followed my choice, every single woman in my family followed suit. Then this confidence seemed to spread like wildfire through my circle of friends. Dozens of them called me and asked for advice and encouragement on how they could do the same.

Do you see what God was doing? He was taking what He'd naturally given me and was using it as a way of speaking to the hearts of women around me about the uniqueness of their natural beauty too. He'd brought me back to an appreciation and acceptance of the stained glass He'd originally put in my window—which He'd put there *on purpose*—and He was shining His light through that particular pane so that it caught other people's attention and made them desire again what He had given them.

That's pretty cool to me.

Now, thankfully, today, for women of all colors, wearing our hair in its natural state has become more universally accepted and celebrated. Still, though, it's a point of pressure for a lot of people. I can't tell you how many times someone has stopped me—just out in public, total strangers—and made comments about my hair, even to the point of insisting on putting their hands on it and touching it. Usually they're already touching it before they ask.

I know. Weird. Hair can just be such a big deal.

But I don't think I've ever been happier about the choice I made with my hair than after I was offered the opportunity to be an actress in the 2015 film *War Room*. As you can imagine, like anyone who puts themselves in the public eye, the feedback I received from that performance ran the gamut of criticism and congratulations. But among the most special (and perhaps the most frequent) letters and comments and e-mails I received were from African American girls, from African American young women, women who look like me and thanked me for presenting a role model of someone who accepted and relished and embraced my own natural hair. It gave them courage to do the same.

Each time I open one of those pieces of correspondence—still today—from a twelve-year-old girl or a thirty-year-old woman writing to tell me she feels encouraged to be herself because she saw *me* being myself, it thrills me . . . especially as I think back to the rigors of that decision I made years earlier, which (believe me) was gut-wrenchingly hard to make at the time.

What if I'd delayed? What if I'd been too afraid, too tentative, too slow to make a break from the sameness? What if I'd felt stuck with what someone else said I needed to be, by what society said was necessary for me to be considered pretty or presentable, acceptable, professional? If I'd waited, I wouldn't have been ready to be a witness to the *wonders* of my individuality. I wouldn't have been such a stark testimony to the creativity of my Father in making me uniquely me. My fear of taking a different path—the uniqueness of my path as a young black woman—would've wasted precious years that God knew I needed for what He knew He was planning for me.

And let me tell you something. I don't want that kind of fear to block anything from you.

So again, I ask you: What's your story? And what will *become* your story? What are the parts of your physical body that just don't seem right to you, that you wish were different, the parts that don't fit in with the prescribed pattern of beauty in your family? In your school? On your team? In your neighborhood? In your country? When you see yourself in comparison to others, when you measure yourself against the prettier physical package that you think other people possess, where do you feel as though you come up short?

Have you considered just letting that part of you . . . be *you?* Instead of masking it or hiding it—instead of working around it so others don't notice it—instead of chemically altering it or doing whatever's required to change it—what if you just owned and embraced it? Whatever it is?

I know you're just reading along here, and I don't want to slow you down, but . . . well, okay, maybe I do, because I want you to just pause for a moment and spend some time applying the lessons of my story to yours. Think through questions like these:

- What aspect of your physique are you changing or hiding in hopes of fitting in?
- What, if anything, are you sacrificing (emotionally, spiritually, or physically) to do this?
- Is fitting in more important to you than your own happiness, health, or honoring God?
- By trying to change this part of who you are, how are you also changing your influence?
- What are some of the losses of not being yourself?
- How could these losses grow worse in the future?
- What would feel the most freeing about being who you are?

At one point or another, each of us feels this same distress about her physical body and its attributes to some degree. We're all more attuned and sensitive to things about ourselves that we find ugly or unwanted. But your significance is not found in how others perceive you and whether or not they accept you. Your value doesn't rely on their applause. You are made in the image of God Himself. And His Word says, "Your body is a temple of the Holy Spirit who is in you, whom you have from God" (1 Corinthians 6:19). As a believer in Christ, your body is valuable enough to be His home and emit His light. It's breathtaking! It's all a planned opportunity for Him to put His light on display. Through you.

So no matter how you *feel,* this truth is who you *are.*

Obviously, this means you should take good care of your body. It deserves your attention in treating it with nutritious food and exercise and whatever kinds of good habits contribute to its overall strength and stature. Each of us is responsible for being good stewards of our bodies, improving our health in any areas where we've not managed it well. And we can feel good about the style preferences we choose that make our look unique to our personalities.

But there's a difference between seeing the need to take wholesome care of yourself and being embarrassed about your innate design. There's a difference between working to strengthen your body in certain spots, as opposed to unnaturally and dangerously trying to morph it into something else.

For instance, my nineteen-year-old neighbor, Kimberley, spent most of her high school career as a competitive gymnast. She longed for that kind of coveted body, as well as the triumph of succeeding in high-level gymnastics. And, man, she went after it—into that world where the only thing the judges want to see on a young woman's body are skin, muscle, and bone. But Kimberley's body type was not naturally rail thin. Keeping it svelte and slender—at *that* level of svelte and slender—was not really achievable through healthy, balanced nutrition. Only through starving.

And so that's what she did. She starved herself. At her coach's unspoken pressure, she chose to work *against* the body that God had given her, forcing it to conform to an arbitrary standard, as well as to her own willful desire to become a champion in a particular sport. Not until her eyes opened to what she was doing and how she was harming herself did she realize the danger she'd invited. The competitive drive God had placed inside her was real and good and authentic, something she felt called to use and act upon. But she found a way to channel it into *another* sport where she could maintain performance without sacrificing health. The body type that had been a liability in gymnastics was exactly ideal for how she needed to perform in this new one. Thankfully, the Lord matched her with the kind of coach who saw her stature as an asset and helped her understand how to take care of it, value it, and maximize its potential. And she excelled.

See, your body is telling you something—even the parts you wish would shut up, go away, or be different somehow. The unique physical components that come together to create *you* are central to the purpose and plan that you were made for. Nothing is *wrong* with you. Nothing is wasted on you. It all matters. Relax and let God show you what He had in mind for you all along when He made you.

Someone else is waiting to have her confidence fostered by your courage to be yourself—in your body, with your hair, relaxed in your own personality, accepting of your own struggles and weaknesses, expectant about how God intends to use it all for His glory.

So . . . what's your story?

I can tell you without a doubt that it's got the makings of a God-story.

4

MAKING OF A MIRACLE

I went to the University of Houston and met Jessica during my first week on campus. She was a sophomore and already ingrained into active college life. I followed her example, joining her as a member of the school's gospel choir and also in a sorority. I liked her as soon as I met her. She struck me as unique for many reasons, but one of them was her unique physical appearance.

Jessica is American born, through and through, but her facial features resemble the heritage of previous ancestors from an indigenous, aboriginal tribe in another part of the world. As our friendship grew, she confided in me that the size of her nose and the overall shape and height of her body, noticeably different from most others, had been fodder for merciless teasing as a young girl. (I can relate to that.) She basically endured ridicule throughout all her growing-up years for what she deemed her unfortunate appearance.

One summer, while classes were out of session, Jessica went on her first short-term mission trip. After nearly twenty-four hours of exhausting travel, the team to which she was attached arrived at a remote town, then began walking deeper into the area where they would be serving. As she and her group approached the village, children started to run enthusiastically toward them. Not really to *them* exactly, but to *her.* They all ran straight to Jessica, clinging to her with hugs and cheers. They said hello to the others, but with a noticeable sense of timidity and stiffness. With Jessica, however, the connection was immediate.

She looked down into the faces of these beautiful children from a tribe halfway across the world, then looked up into the faces of their mothers, who were beginning to walk up slowly toward her . . . and she saw it. She realized what was happening.

She *looked* like them; they looked like *her.* That face, those cheekbones, that nose, every bit of her physical countenance fit in immediately. Of all the members on that particular ministry team, none was received or heard or given more credence by the people who lived in those villages than Jessica. They related primarily with *her.* They listened most attentively to *her.* They felt the most natural relationship with *her.* Because she *looked* like them. Her unique creation was the stained glass she'd been intentionally fitted with by God for such a time as this . . . to walk into the lives and hearts of those people at that time in that place.

The design, you see—your design, my design—it all makes perfect sense from God's perspective. Which means, if we'll only listen to Him and believe Him, it should start to make more sense to us as well.

I don't know how old or young you are. But it's time—today—for you to accept and resonate with the young woman God has made you to be. The sooner, the better . . . because my distinctions, your distinctions, are truly wonders.

Miracles, actually . . .

Look closer at Psalm 139, and you'll see a miracle story woven into it. God says you've been "remarkably and wondrously made." But what does that really mean?

The Hebrew word translated as "wondrous" or "wonderful" in Psalm 139:14 (AMP) actually appears in a number of different places throughout the Old Testament. And it means something totally miraculous. Looking at this same concept in different contexts can widen how you understand the gravity and wonder of who God says He's fashioned you to be.

In Exodus 3, for instance, God Himself appeared to Moses somewhere out in the desert. The Israelites at this time had been enslaved in Egypt for hundreds of years. And through the awesomeness of a burning bush, God spoke to Moses and said:

> *"When I stretch out my hand and strike*
> *Egypt with all my miracles that I will*
> *perform in it, after that, he [the Egyptian*
> *pharaoh] will let you go."* (EXODUS 3:20)

These "miracles" would be the plagues that eventually drove Pharaoh to give the ancient Israelites their freedom. Each one was a *wonder*, a distinct reflection of the power of God. It was *wonderful* what God did there, the *miracles* He unleashed in all His supernatural glory. Not even the greatest empire on the face of the earth could withstand the demonstration of His incredible might when He determined to rescue His people.

Look at the power of God's wondrous miracles and the impact they had here. They inspired one ordinary man (Moses) to become an instrument of change and a liberator for others. They brought the real-time enemy of God's people (Egypt's pharaoh) into alignment with God's plan. Even greater, they freed a massive number of people (more than two million Hebrews) from their captors, enabling them to experience a new, divine encounter with God. This is what your life has the potential to do too—inspiring people who see His reflection in you to want the freedom and abundance He offers.

God's miracles are just that *wondrous.*

And the word used in Scripture to describe those miracles—to tell you *what they were* in Exodus 3—is the same word used in Scripture to describe you—*who you are*—in Psalm 139.

You are *wondrous.*

After the children of Israel were freed from Egypt and began their trek through the wilderness, God continued the work He had started in them. He divided the Red Sea so they could walk safely across (Exodus 14:26–31). He satiated their hunger with quail and manna from heaven (16:11–15). He quenched their thirst with water from a rock (17:5–6). *Miracle* after *miracle* after *miracle.* Finally, they reached the same mountain where God had first spoken to Moses from the burning bush—the same mountain He'd promised they would one day gather around to worship Him as an entire body of people. And there the Lord said:

> *"I will perform wonders in the presence of all*
> *your people that have never been done in the*
> *whole earth or in any nation. All the people you*
> *live among will see the LORD's work, for what I am*
> *doing with you is awe-inspiring."* (EXODUS 34:10)

"I will perform wonders," He said . . . like no one's ever seen before. And that's exactly what He did. The miraculous crossing of the Jordan River (Joshua 3:15–17). The walls of Jericho crumbling to the ground as the Israelites marched around them, shouting and blowing their trumpets (Joshua 6:20). In place after place, God empowered the ragtag forces of Israel to conquer entrenched enemies throughout the entire land of Canaan—this new homeland He had pledged to give to His people as their permanent possession.

It's amazing what God did for them. It was *wondrous.*

And it's amazing what He's done in you.

You're not unimportant—you're *wondrous.*

You're not unacceptable—you're *wondrous.*

You're not a waste of effort—you're *wondrous.*

Stop and realize what a remarkable miracle you are. And like all God's miracles, you were created to have a ripple effect of inexplicable and astounding impact.

In the exodus, God planned (then performed) specific, extraordinary, miraculous acts that were so unique, so eye-opening, so jaw-dropping that no human being could ever replicate them or remain unaffected by them. They changed the fate of Moses. They changed the fate of the children of Israel. They even changed the fate of their worst enemies.

And the *wonderful word* that describes what He did through His *wonderful works* back then is the same word that describes how "wondrously" He made *you!*

You will spend your whole life either (1) comparing and competing, trying to be and become something you were never meant to be, or (2) accepting your uniqueness for what it is—a miracle worth celebrating and displaying, an identity and purpose you can invest your whole self into.

The first option is exhausting, frustrating, and soul killing, marked by crippling perfectionism, fear, and insecurity. The second, however, is lined with enjoyment, freedom, and fulfillment—not only for you but for the people you encounter.

Why?

Because then His light is able to shine through the prism of your uniqueness, and the people in your world will see Him.

They're waiting.

What are *you* waiting for?

5

THE SAME, ONLY DIFFERENT

Did you know that the small of your back has about a million tiny hairs on it? I didn't know this incidental fact either until one excruciating night when I made a most painful discovery.

Around my junior year of high school, my parents planted the seed in my mind that if I wanted to go to the college of my choice, I would need to seek out scholarship money anywhere I could possibly find it. Through our school guidance counselor and others, I learned about several ways to apply for money to cover the cost of books, tuition, and everything, with the hopes of securing a full ride into college. I wrote essays. I sent in reference letters. I sat through interviews with university admissions personnel.

I was on a mission. Whatever it took.

At some point, a lady from our church suggested the idea of entering a scholarship pageant. The groups that sponsored them awarded scholarship money as part of their prize package. HA! As if I were the beauty pageant contestant type. All the ones I'd seen on television and in magazines were startlingly gorgeous, not with faces like mine, which was mercilessly covered in acne. And they were skinny. They were stick skinny. My own build by contrast had always tended toward being more athletic. Huskier. Heavier. I just couldn't fathom the idea of putting my muscular frame on display for people to analyze and criticize.

"But it's not all about physical appearance," the lady told me. She knew of several local pageants that focused more on the interview and talent portions of the competition than strictly on a girl's looks.

Interviews? (You mean, talking?) I knew I could do that.

Talent? From all my years of gospel choir at church, I thought I could probably sing well enough (or at least *loud* enough) to distract the judges from concentrating on the mounds of pimples on my face, which no amount of concealer could possibly hide.

So I did it. Priscilla Evans became a pageant contender—which is exactly what led me to finding out about all those millions of tiny back hairs I never really knew existed.

Here's how all of that came about. One of the pageants I entered contained a swimsuit segment—not my idea of a good time. But the event was only for a small local group in Dallas, where I lived, which helped me warm up to the idea. As long as it possibly led to more money in my scholarship account, I figured I could tough it out for one night.

But I wasn't very experienced in this type of pageant performance, not like the other girls in the room obviously were. This truth became apparent to me backstage at the theater, where we were dressing. I had quickly changed out of the outfit I'd worn for the talent competition and was starting to put on a deep-orange one-piece for the dreaded swimsuit walk. Suddenly I noticed many of the other girls—the girls more cultured in pageant protocol—tightly wrapping their midsections with a thick blue tape. With each pull, their waists shrank smaller and smaller, as though their body fat was being sucked out by a vacuum hose. It was amazing. I *needed* some of that stuff. If I had any prayer of winning this thing, I needed to do what everybody else was doing.

Unfortunately, though, I didn't know duct tape (or whatever it was) was part of a pageant girls' toolkit. I hadn't thought to pack any of my own. But feeling the pressure to conform, I dared to ask one of the girls near me—you know, kind of nonchalantly—if I could borrow some of her tape. Did she mind? Because I was fresh out . . .

She tossed the roll my way, and I commenced to wrapping. Starting at my belly button, I peeled it four or five times around my body, yanking harder on the tape with each pass. By the end, I'd plastered a blue-tape corset about six inches wide around my lower torso, and I could hardly breathe. My diaphragm was just gasping for air. I'd never felt so constricted and uncomfortable in my life. But, hey, I looked like the other girls now.

So whatever.

I got through the walk of swimsuit shame. It had been hard to take full, deep breaths, but I'd gutted it out. Or, more accurately, gutted it in. When I walked off the stage and hustled back behind the curtain, I hurriedly began my transition toward the final part of the show, the evening gown competition.

That's when my problems really began.

I quickly shimmied into my long formal gown, just as I'd done when trying it on at the store. Then I spun around to look at myself from all angles in the mirror. The dress looked as gorgeous as it had looked when I'd picked it out . . . except for one totally unforeseen consequence. I hadn't accounted for the fact that my dress, which featured a V-shaped back, didn't cover that six-inch swatch of garish torture tape. My dress was black and gold . . . with a new accent of royal blue above the waistline!

And I only had a few seconds to get rid of it.

I didn't think twice. I pinched at one end of the tape, curling it up with my fingernails, trying to separate it from my skin. But it was stuck like glue, all around my body. I yanked and felt an unexpected pain, shooting like fire up the small of my back. I'd barely pulled off a quarter inch, and the searing sting it left behind on my tender flesh made me think I was never getting this tape off in time. Not without leaving burn marks. Or drawing blood.

I could feel my stress level rising. Beads of sweat dotted my forehead. I was panicked. I batted back the tears that threatened to streak my perfectly applied makeup as I tried pulling off another inch. The pain was excruciating—the little hairs zinging like a thousand tiny needles on my skin. There was no way I'd be able to unwrap this tape in time to go back on. It just hurt too badly.

A kind attendant had been posted backstage to monitor our situation and see if any of us girls needed help. Spying my dilemma, this woman appeared at my chair with a wide-eyed look of knowing concern on her face and a parted pair of scissors in her hands. She stood behind me and carefully sliced through the tape. Starting from the top (which was about midway up my back), she was able to make a complete V-shaped incision to match the line of my dress. I was now wearing a wide belt of tape around my midsection, broken only by this ragged gash in the rear. Then with a cursory warning to "hold your breath, dear," that sweet, gentle lady ripped the big blue Band-Aid from my back with one mighty pull, and—I kid you not—I thought for a second I would pass out.

Did you know the small of your back has about a million tiny hairs on it? (Have I asked you that question already?) Trust me: it does. I just hope you never have to find out for yourself. At least not like that! It was torturous.

But I also hope you never have to feel that same pain in another way—in an emotional way.

Ask me how I know . . .

I can't tell you how many women I've met, well into their thirties or forties or fifties, who are feeling the pain of undoing what they did in their teen years. They stuffed their beautifully unique, God-given personality into a mold that their peer group found more appealing. They could hardly breathe from the tight cocoon of comparison, the rigid, narrow box that suffocated their inner selves—their unique interests, quirks, and temperament. Their significance was so tightly bound to the approval of others that they didn't have the courage to break free and be proudly individual, to be who God had made them to be on the inside.

Years later, though, they grew tired of gasping for air. And so, they started to pull at the tape. Rediscovering their passions. Revisiting old interest areas. Reacquainting themselves with who they were created to be. And let me tell you, it's been a harrowing process. It's taken a long time. And sometimes it's taken lots of help. They've needed wise counselors to carefully slice through the fears and insecurities that bind them, helping pull the trappings painfully away.

Know why I'm telling you this? Because you, little sister, have a chance to chart a different path. Right now, at this stage in your life, you can make choices that let you avoid the emotional ripping and tearing that's happening all over the female world tonight. I want to spare you that experience.

That's why I want to help you grab hold of some truths that will cut you away from unnecessary bondage and set you free.

You are an incredible catalog of physical uniqueness, personality traits, passionate interests, past experiences, and other peculiarities handcrafted by almighty God. They're *you*. They're part of what makes you so unique. Along the road of life, you'll be tempted to mute these details and squeeze them into a culturally acceptable container. Instead of just being yourself—courageous, cautious, quiet, inquisitive, whatever— you'll be enticed to chameleon yourself into whatever the situation expects of you, if that's how everybody's apparently supposed to do it.

But if that person is not *you,* you'll end up binding your real self into a straitjacket, suffocating in silence, as you try (unsuc- cessfully) to gain the approval of people or to find your worth in achievement and success. You'll stop being yourself, stop pursuing your passions, stop letting the world see something else besides another Exhibit A, monolithic, totally predict- able, copycat cutout. And who needs another one of those? Especially when there's you!

And you're wonderful!

The stage of life needs all the players on it, each one doing her part and affirming others as they do theirs. But if you're busy trying to play someone else, who's going to play you? You'll leave a gaping hole, sis, that can't be filled without you.

The whole reason I found myself in that precarious pageant predicament was because I was determined to fit in. I'd stuffed myself into a mold. And although the shudder of having heavy- duty tape adhesive savagely torn from your back is not an expe- rience I recommend or desire to repeat, the truth is, we volunteer for all kinds of painful consequences every time we make an assembly-line attempt to look and be like everybody else.

And yet that's what most of us do because sameness is all too celebrated in our society. Oh, you don't hear it *said* like that. People say, "Be yourself, girl. You do you." But often that's not what they mean. That's not how the system works. Uniqueness is only valued to the extent that it stays within the uniform boundaries of prescribed sameness. If you dare to have morals that align with God's truth, if you choose to buck the set standards of beauty and success, you'll be threatened with silent exclusion from your peers. Honoring the young woman God made you to be by living in a way that glorifies Him and respecting the way He made you requires a thick skin.

Now, sure, if you stuff everything down inside, you may succeed at minimizing risk and exposure. You may avoid needing to answer so many questions or explain yourself. But you'll also deaden your passion for many of the things you like and love and feel called of God to be. That's a terrible tradeoff.

But it's the enemy's way. The devil wants to make you question your identity. Hide it. Mute it. Compartmentalize it. Keep it to yourself. Don't offer it up to the light, where others can see it and possibly make fun of it, where they can judge you, pick at you, pigeonhole you. Don't be *too* unique. It's bad for business.

I promise you, though—later in life, when you want to breathe again, you'll have to pull that tape. It's the only way out. And the longer the tape stays on you, the more it hurts to remove.

Why not just be your God-honoring self *now?* Why wait? For what?

Seriously, what are you waiting for?

That makes me think of my niece Kariss. She's all grown up now. Has a handsome husband and two gorgeous kids. She also runs her own photography business. (Her Instagram feed is almost beautiful enough to eat!) And she can generally do anything creative, artistic, crafty. What a fun young woman she's grown up to be.

Looking at her today, you're amazed. Want to see the light of God shining through her life? There it is. It's in the impeccable lighting and composition of those pictures she takes. It's in the color and creativity of her latest home renovation project. It's in the way she carries herself and tells you what's most important in her life. Anybody can see it. Easy.

But back when Kariss was in school—back when she was closer to your age—a person might have looked at her and seen only a young woman who didn't fit in. She was never quite uniform. She didn't learn like everybody else. She didn't have the same interests as everybody else. Her capacity for things like staying organized, for making straight As—you know, for *math* and stuff—it just wasn't going to happen.

I can tell you from personal observation: she did her best at those things. She really did. But I can also tell you something else, and it's the part I most want you to hear. She did it without berating herself for being different from those who excelled in the more academic, more percentile-graded, more customary measures of teenage progress. Instead, she dared to walk her own path, the one that fostered the things she was actually good at doing, the one that gave her an opportunity to pursue her real interests. Like sewing. Graphic design. Photography. Yeah, she signed up for actual classes in those subjects, even during her high school years.

Because it's how God made her.

It's how His light shines best through her.

As I watch her gifts exploding now—in her photography career, her social media presence, her beauty as a wife and mother—I can't help but wonder how much the world would have missed if she'd dulled her unique design. Makes me sad to think of what *I* would have missed. What if she'd decided she couldn't risk being herself? What if she'd succumbed to the pressure to conform and streamline? What if she'd looked at the stained glass window of her life and concluded that these details were just too different, too oddly constructed, that she needed to seriously tone down the prism effect created by her naturally created uniqueness? What if she'd chosen a cookie-cutter take on coolness and popularity and decided she didn't want to wake up in the morning if she couldn't be more like everybody else?

Most likely, she wouldn't be the Kariss I know and love today. More important, she wouldn't be the Kariss that *she* knows and loves today. Instead she'd be expending precious time and energy ripping at that compression tape she'd wound around herself as a younger woman, hoping against hope that there was still something left inside of the uniquely beautiful person she'd been stuffing down deeper and deeper all her life.

Possible. But painful.

Set yourself free right now, while the tape roll is there in your hand and you're considering whether or not to start wrapping yourself in it. *Don't do it.* You are a wonder, just the way God made you. You are a miracle, with all your one-of-a-kind originality. You are the girl He created you to be. And this alone makes you special. And necessary.

So tilt the window. Catch the light. Reflect His radiance.

And unleash the wonder.

The world is waiting . . . *on you.*

TO THINK ABOUT

- Which aspects of your physical body do you struggle the most to appreciate and feel good about?
- Which aspects of your personality do you most struggle to accept and appreciate?
- Knowing that you are a "temple" of God's Spirit, how does this fact adjust the way you take care of yourself and view your inherent value?
- Who is someone you know whose confidence in her God-given uniqueness inspires you to celebrate your own?

TO TAKE AWAY

When considering making changes to your physical appearance (different hairstyle, different makeup, different clothes) . . . *pause*. Check with yourself. Question your motivation. Determine why. Maybe your honest answers will lead you toward certain choices but away from others.

God's creative genius is reflected in you. Make a gratitude list of your unique internal and external features that you want to thank Him for. Ask Him to help you value what He esteems in you.

Consider the fact that you were created with a divine mission in mind. Ask the Lord to begin to open your eyes to the way your uniqueness is matched with the assignment He's got in mind for you.

PART TWO

FROM DARKNESS TO LIGHT

Read This

God who said, "Let light shine out of darkness," has shone in our hearts to give the light of the knowledge of God's glory in the face of Jesus Christ. (2 CORINTHIANS 4:6)

Say This

In Christ, I am fully, finally alive. I am chosen by God, accepted as His child, and forgiven of every sin. I am His daughter, and His light is not just behind me; His light is in me. This means I'm not confined by my limitations. My weaknesses are not liabilities. Instead, as an accepted and surrendered child of God, my whole self is a platform for His glory to be displayed. I am who He says I am. I can do what He says I can do. In Him, I can become everything He says I can become.

Believe This

In him was life, and that life was the light of men. That light shines in the darkness, and yet the darkness did not overcome it. (JOHN 1:4-5)

6

MATTERS OF LIFE AND DEATH

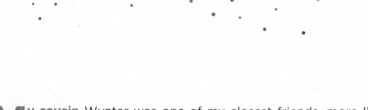

My cousin Wynter was one of my closest friends, more like a biological sister than a distant relative. She was the best friend who joined me at the movies for an impromptu girls' night or for dinner at a local restaurant. Whenever anything funny or scary or difficult happened in my life, she was one of the first people I'd call to laugh about it, celebrate it, cry over it, or filter it through. We took vacations together, raised our children together, and even mapped out our plans for the kind of future we each envisioned for the next season of our lives.

Which is why it came as such a devastating shock—July 24, 2018—when her heart just suddenly stopped beating.

She was only thirty-eight.

So sudden. So shocking. She'd been fine earlier that day—braiding her daughters' hair, playing board games with her sister-in-law and nieces, making plans to see a movie with me the following day. Her last message to me was at 5:15 in the afternoon before going to lie down and take a little nap. A nap that she never woke up from.

Her body just gave out. And her husband, as well as the paramedics who responded to his 911 call, could do nothing to help her.

Several days later, as family and friends gathered, four of us women were tasked with arriving an hour or so ahead of everyone else at the funeral home to make sure Wynter's body looked presentable before the viewing at her service. I don't know how else to say it: she still looked beautiful, even in her casket. A beautician had coiffed her hair. A makeup artist had meticulously cared for her face. She was wearing a gorgeous dress and dainty jewelry.

But here's what we all know.

No amount of hairstyling or makeup or nice clothes or accessories were able to put breath back into my sweet friend's body. She wouldn't be calling and leaving messages on my phone anymore.

Wynter was dead.

And death cannot be undone by outward adornments and postmortem modifications, no matter how beautifully you dress it up.

*   *   *   *   *   *   *
*   *   *   *

You were dead in your trespasses and sins
in which you previously lived according to
the ways of this world. (EPHESIANS 2:1-2)

I want to reaffirm to you, before we go any further, what I've been telling you all along. You are a beautiful expression of God's creative genius. You have been carefully, personally crafted by your Maker with intentionality and uniqueness. Nothing ever changes that. He made you special, for special purposes.

But there's a difference between being His creation and being His child. There's a difference between having the biological apparatus to function within earth's atmosphere and having the spiritual transformation to be able to live and love Him throughout all eternity.

What I'm saying is: a whole lot of pretty, put-together, full-of-potential people who you pass every day are in reality dead women walking—"dead" in their sins—blinded to the fact that they need to be made "alive with Christ" (Ephesians 2:5). He "wants everyone to be saved and to come to the knowledge of the truth," and has given Himself "as a ransom for all" (1 Timothy 2:4, 6). But not everyone will listen to His Word or see the reality of their need for Him. Instead, perfectly applied makeup and high-end fashion will mask the rigor mortis that makes its mark on their souls.

In other words: It's one thing to be born, and it's an entirely other thing to be "born again" (John 3:3). There's being created, and there's being a "new creation" (2 Corinthians 5:17). And if we stop short of receiving this new life from Him—by putting our faith in what Jesus Christ did on the cross to forgive and redeem us—we are certifiably, spiritually dead, even while we live.

Dead inside.

It's all because something terrible happened—something terribly significant—at the beginning of time in the garden of Eden. The enemy, Satan, challenged the perfection of our first parents' creation by saying to Eve, "You surely will not die," if she chose to sin against God's commands and doubt His heart of love for her (Genesis 3:4 NASB). But immediately after she and Adam made their prideful decision to eat of the forbidden fruit, desiring to be their own God, they realized their shame and the separation it caused in their relationship with Him. They ran and hid. Tried to cover up. They did what we, their children, would be born to do: to hide from God, to fear His nearness, to resist the love and protection found in His commands.

> *Just as sin entered the world through one man,*
> *and death through sin, in this way death spread*
> *to all people, because all sinned.* (ROMANS 5:12)

So even though you and I are "remarkably and wondrously made"—which is still true!—we arrived here with a problem that only God could remedy. Being spiritually dead means there's nothing we can do to change what these "trespasses and sins" have done to our hearts. We may be able to *improve* in areas where we're frustrated with ourselves. We may be able to *tweak* some of the influences and relationships and lifestyle patterns that contribute to our struggles. But death is incurable. Death stays dead.

Even when you put makeup on it.

Only by believing in Jesus can you experience the one miracle that's greater than the miracle of your creation—the wonder that makes even the wonder of your precious human life appear pale by comparison. Only through Jesus can you experience resurrection.

Life from death.

> *He died for all so that those who live should no*
> *longer live for themselves, but for the one who*
> *died for them and was raised.* (2 CORINTHIANS 5:15)

Light from the darkness.

> *"Anyone who follows me will never walk in the*
> *darkness but will have the light of life."* (JOHN 8:12)

Transformed from God's creation to God's own child.

> *To all who did receive him, he gave them*
> *the right to be children of God, to those who*
> *believe in his name, who were born, not of*
> *natural descent, or of the will of the flesh, or*
> *of the will of man, but of God.* (JOHN 1:12–13)

In Jesus, the Bible says, you can be brought to life. You don't have to be dead anymore—a hollow shell.

Pretty but empty.

Impressive but unfulfilled.

Instead, in Christ, you can come to life and be rooted in eternal significance that's not subject to the fickle approval of other people. You can find meaning and purpose, and *truly* reflect His light. Every day. For the rest of your life.

7

LOOK AT YOU NOW

In the movie *Overcomer,* my character—school principal Olivia Brooks—takes a personal interest in one particular student, a young ninth grader named Hannah. Olivia is aware of some of Hannah's life circumstances and the more unique, difficult challenges she's facing. For one thing, both her parents are dead (or so she's been told), and she's being raised by her stoic grandmother. She struggles in school, suffers from asthma, and mostly keeps to herself—basically doesn't play well with others. She feels empty, invisible, and insecure. And in an effort to find the significance she feels is lacking, she has resorted to inappropriate behaviors and attitudes.

She is spiraling out of control.

One day at school, Olivia grabs an opportunity to engage Hannah in private conversation. She senses that Hannah is hurting, even though there isn't an obvious need that she can put her finger on, like trouble in math or history class. There's just a void, an emptiness—something intangible that Ms. Brooks detects. It's an internal, personal crisis that needs attention.

Hannah is struggling to understand who she is.

Soon their conversation about school subjects and track practice begins drifting toward spiritual things. And as Hannah opens up about some of her own battles and questions, the tenderhearted principal explains the gospel to her and asks if she'd like to receive Jesus as her Savior. In one of the sweeter, more touching moments of the film, Olivia clasps hands with Hannah, and the two of them pray together.

You may be interested to know that the words of that prayer were not actually in the script. The director told me to lead Hannah using the same words I'd pray with anyone who I was sitting or standing beside in real life. Here's the prayer that I'd say, whether I'm playing a character named Olivia or just as regular ol' Priscilla, locking hands and hearts with you through the pages of a book . . .

Lord Jesus,
I am a sinner.
And I need a Savior.
I believe that you are that Savior.
So today, I place faith alone, in Christ
alone, to forgive my sins.
Come live in me.
In Jesus' name,
Amen.

I hope you've prayed similar words yourself and believed these life-changing realities—whether many years ago or maybe right this minute as you're reading. If so, like Hannah's in the movie, your identity has been transformed. You've become a new creation.

Listen to me . . .

You are brand-new.

You haven't only been changed; you've been *exchanged.*

You've been transferred from the kingdom of darkness into the kingdom of light and life.

Your identity is rooted in the fact that God the Father has adopted you as His child.

Now as you grow in your relationship with Christ and become increasingly aware of your new identity and inheritance, your whole life will become a reflection of your new status. This means that even though all your problems don't magically change, the way you handle them and respond to them and react to them changes, because *you've* changed.

Living a life that is congruent with your new identity, one that draws on your new and lavish spiritual inheritance, changes everything.

That's why Olivia gave Hannah an assignment—the same assignment I want to give you in real life. Over the next week or two, I encourage you to read the first two chapters of a Bible book called Ephesians, a letter from the apostle Paul to a first-century church. Here in these few hundred words is perhaps a more concentrated look at your new identity and inheritance in Christ than anywhere else in Scripture, spelled out in one incredible statement after another—bam, bam, bam. Take only a few verses each day, if you like, stopping to prayerfully think about what each of these promises from God to you really means. What you'll discover is that these passages have the power to change your whole life . . .

- the way you think and respond;
- the choices you make;
- the outlook you maintain;
- the perspectives you choose;
- the behaviors you act on.

The statements you'll read about your new identity in Ephesians 1–2 are not just a bunch of spiritual-sounding phrases that don't really matter or affect your life every day. They're the truth of God's Word—the gavel-down, absolute truth about *who you are* and *what you have*—ready to help you wade into any of those places where you're tempted or mistreated or made to feel less-than, and be able to stand there confident in God's own assessment of you, *knowing* who you are and what you have access to. They'll keep you from misplacing your identity in illegitimate relationships or vain pursuits or unfulfilling ambitions. They'll solidify your worth and significance in the right place so you won't venture off looking for them in the wrong places.

Mind if I introduce you? May I tell you a little about yourself?

You are **CHOSEN**.

> *He chose us in him [in Christ], before the*
> *foundation of the world, to be holy and*
> *blameless in love before him.* (EPHESIANS 1:4)

Chosen. You aren't just a kid God somehow got stuck with. You have been "adopted" (v. 5) into His family—not as a last-minute selection, but chosen "before the foundation of the world." God has always known you, has always had plans for you. He chose you to be a young woman who would put your trust in Him, would surrender yourself to His Word and His plans for you, and would show others what happens when someone allows herself to be transformed by Christ's life. He *chose* you for this position. He has always wanted you here. You are *His*.

You are **FORGIVEN**.

> *In him we have redemption through his blood,*
> *the forgiveness of our trespasses, according*
> *to the riches of his grace.* (EPHESIANS 1:7)

Forgiven. It's the one-word difference between heaven and hell. It means that whatever you've done, or are doing, or will ever do that doesn't start and end with faith will not be held against you. Which means the burden of guilt and shame is *off* of you. You're free of it. Because you're *forgiven.* What does that kind of person, living that kind of reality, do with the rest of her day today? (HINT: not sin like she's been given a blank check.) She receives her guilt-free pass as the unfathomable gift she knows it to be, and rather than being enslaved to sin any longer, she starts asking, "How can I spread this gift of forgiveness around to others today?" Our forgiveness cost Jesus His life. Which means we should never be able to take it casually as if it's not a big deal. Instead, the reality that we are free and have been cleared of the penalty we deserve should make us come nearly unglued in gratitude. The price has already been paid. It is finished.

You are **ACCEPTED**.

> *He made us accepted in the Beloved.* (EPHESIANS 1:6 NKJV)

Accepted. A girl who knows she's already loved and accepted doesn't succumb to the chase, to the maddening, never-ending pursuit of getting others to approve of her. She doesn't exhaust herself trying to find her value in people's acceptance. As a beloved daughter of the Most High God, she already knows she's loved and accepted more fully and unconditionally than any other person on earth could ever love and accept her. She realizes that when the Father looks at her, He sees her through the flawless prism of Jesus' perfect sacrifice on the cross. And because *that* was enough, *she* is enough. So she rests, knowing that because of Christ she is "holy and blameless in love before him" (v. 4). Her drive to achieve and accomplish things is not based on gaining acceptance anymore, since she's already got that. It's simply the fruit of her gratitude for all that her Father has done. She lives to make

His name great and fulfill her assignment. She doesn't have anything to prove. She doesn't succumb to the paralysis of perfectionism. She can relax in her status as a beloved daughter. Every weakness, every flaw, every struggle. As is. Because she is totally and completely accepted.

You have an eternal **INHERITANCE***.*

In him we have also received an inheritance, because we were predestined according to the plan of the one who works out everything in agreement with the purpose of his will. (EPHESIANS 1:11)

Inheritance. You are the beneficiary of more blessings and bounty than your heart and hands could ever hold. And unlike a child who may receive a financial legacy that's left to her for later use, the "inheritance" Paul described in Ephesians doesn't just come with a priceless, eternal payoff for later. You have access to it right now. You can draw spiritual dividends from it this afternoon during math class or piano lessons. This benefits package includes "every spiritual blessing" you could possibly be given (Ephesians 1:3); the "full armor of God" for use in standing up against and defeating the enemy (6:11); and a seat with Christ "in the heavenly places," where you are already victorious in every area of your life (2:6 NASB). Your God has lavishly, abundantly provided for your spiritual care and coverage. There's no need to scrimp and cut corners and count your change to be sure you'll have enough love, acceptance, grace, freedom, forgiveness, and victory from Him in your bank account by the end of the week. No need to question whether the reserves you need for patience, power, or equipping are available to help you accomplish the tasks set before you. In Him, there is no lack or scarcity. Everything you need is already part of your inheritance.

You have the **POWER** *of Christ in you.*

. . . the immeasurable greatness of his power
toward us who believe, according to the mighty
working of his strength. (EPHESIANS 1:19)

Power. God's supernatural strength and fortitude proved so mighty and so formidable that not even death could stop it. It was a power so, well . . . *powerful* . . . that it raised Jesus from the dead after His crucifixion. How's that for power? But listen to this: it's the same power that's now been given to you. The Holy Spirit indwells you, giving you the capacity to live beyond your natural abilities. As a result of your salvation, you've been "sealed" by His presence in your life (Ephesians 1:13), which means you are covered. You are protected left, right, and sideways for today, tomorrow, and forever. The Holy Spirit is the "down payment of our inheritance" (v. 14)—living there in your heart, reminding you that you are a child of God, and giving you access to all the power and strength you need, not only to survive, but to thrive.

You have **FULL ACCESS** *to God.*

Now in Christ Jesus, you who were far
away have been brought near by the
blood of Christ. (EPHESIANS 2:13)

Access. God has done more astonishing things for us than you or I will ever fully be able to comprehend. But if He did them without giving you access to Him—if He did it like a rich out-of-town relative that you never got to see or talk to or have a real friendship with—something would still be missing. So, although God is indeed high above us, He is not aloof and detached. He wants you to come to Him through prayer and to hear from Him through His Word. He wants to be in a real-time relationship with you, and He offers you a standing open-door policy of interaction. Based on the doorway Jesus has opened for you to the Father, you can "approach the throne of grace with boldness, so that we may receive mercy and find grace to help us in time of need" (Hebrews 4:16). You are welcome in His presence. His dear and precious daughter. Never a bother. Always happy you came.

You are His **DWELLING PLACE**.

In him you are also being built together for God's dwelling in the Spirit. (EPHESIANS 2:22)

His dwelling place. The God who made the entire universe and everything in it, the One who hangs the stars in space and controls the vast arrangement of the galaxies, has chosen a place to live. His home is in *you.* He treasures you so much that as He spans the earth, looking for a suitable place to house His majesty, He chooses you. And me. And this mere fact that He lives in us says something important about us. David said of Him, "Evil cannot dwell with you" (Psalm 5:4). God is holy. He lives only in places that are *holy*—set apart for Him, dedicated to Him, suitable for Him. So would that include you? Yes, the Bible says that *you* are one of those places. You are a prized creation, made "holy and blameless" through what Jesus has done for you (Ephesians 1:4). You're fit for a king. *The* King. Christ dwells in your heart "through faith" (3:17). He wants you to know and believe all these truths about yourself "so that you may be filled with all the fullness of God" (v. 19).

This is *who you are.*

This is *what you have.*

The only question that remains is: *Will you believe it . . . and live like it?*

Back when I was a teenager, I became extremely discouraged because of a girl in my youth group who didn't like me very much. Actually, to tell you the truth, I'm pretty sure she hated me. And it devastated me. I was obsessed with trying to win her approval. I wanted so much for her to like me. For some reason, her validation and acceptance of me really mattered. But all she ever did was brush me off, ignore me, and make me feel small.

My friend Nicole had watched me panic and stew over this for months. She'd had quite enough of seeing me grovel for this girl's affirmation. So one day, Nicole stood in front of me, put her hands on my shoulders, looked me squarely in the eyes, and said these words:

> *Priscilla, not everyone is going to like*
> *you. And that's okay. Their reaction to*
> *you is not a reflection of who you are.*

I've retrieved and replayed those wise words many times throughout my life. *Their reaction is not a reflection of who you are.* Even recently, thirty years after Nicole first said them to me, they bubbled up again to the surface of my conscious stream of thought—just in time to rescue me from sinking into an abyss of disapproval.

Something well-intentioned that I'd said during a Bible study teaching had been spliced out of the video recording and posted on social media. The ninety-second clip, which was not nearly as articulate as I would have wanted it to be, was taken out of context and completely misconstrued. It went viral and angered a lot of people. The glare of scrutiny brought out haters who didn't know me but felt the need to pelt me with insults and insinuations, seeking to slander my character and twist the mission of my family's ministry.

I was in shock as the story mushroomed. Several online news sources began sharing the story and highlighting the controversy, because controversy is always much more enticing than the truth. And even though I'd known that the potential for criticism goes along with the territory of public life, I'd never been caught in the crosshairs of negative attention on such a large scale.

It hurt to be misunderstood so mercilessly, especially when even a large group of my peers with whom I'd always felt connection and community joined the bandwagon of negativity. I felt that old, familiar, unruly desire and angst growing in my heart, as if I were fifteen all over again, desperate to be understood, affirmed, accepted, and vindicated.

During one sleepless night, however, after another cruel stream of tweets had flooded my time line, Nicole's reminder from thirty years ago rang out as confidently and clearly as if she'd just said it to me the night before.

"Their reaction to you"—remember this—*"is not a reflection of who you are."*

I ended up sleeping better that night, because I remembered exactly what I'm praying you will never, ever forget . . .

You are **CHOSEN**.

You are **FORGIVEN**.

You are **ACCEPTED**.

You are **LOVED**.

You have an eternal **INHERITANCE**.

You have the **POWER** of Christ in you.

You have **FULL ACCESS** to God.

You are His **DWELLING PLACE**.

Nobody can ever take that away from you.
Nobody.

8

YOU'RE NEEDED
IN THE KITCHEN

I love hot, salty, buttery popcorn. It's my favorite snack, and I could eat it all the time. Did you know that inside every kernel of popcorn is a microscopic dot of water? Whenever you place a pot of uncooked popcorn on the stove top or in the microwave, the heat penetrates the shell and begins warming it up. The liquid inside the kernel then transforms into steam, and the steam builds in intensity, which creates a growing amount of energy and pressure. When the outer shell is no longer able to handle the pressure that's pushing out against it from the inside—POP!—it explodes. Then all of a sudden, the tiny, hard shell becomes a little flower of fluffy goodness, and I might just eat the entire bowl and leave nothing for *you*. (Just kidding. You can share my popcorn anytime.)

This is a simple but fitting illustration of how God works in your life as a believer, now that He's placed His Holy Spirit inside you. Instead of you working from the outside in—to change yourself—He starts working from the inside out. Because otherwise, nothing changes. Trying to make your behavior reflect your new identity through outside-in methods is like thinking you can create edible popcorn by squeezing on the outer shell. No matter how long and hard you try, you will never get what you're after. The only thing you'll be successful at creating is frustration. You need something (Someone) working and expanding on the inside to see real transformation on the outside. Without the Holy Spirit, you can never become the woman you desire to be.

But when you were reborn with a new identity in Christ, God reversed the polarity on your heart. The Holy Spirit within you (He's part of your new spiritual inheritance, remember—the *best* part) responds to the heat of your prayers, to your willingness to trust His Word, and to your authentic desire for His light to be seen through your life. Then from inside, He starts changing things. Even if you can't see it happening at first, you know the change is coming—because just like with a kernel of popcorn, it's already happening beneath the shell. That hard covering of resistance doesn't have the staying power to keep the Holy Spirit from erupting whenever He chooses, now that you're working together with Him instead of against Him. And when He does—POW!—you never looked so good.

You're not only different on the *inside*; you're deliciously different on the outside.

This progressive, ongoing process of transformation is something you can expect to experience for the rest of your life. It's the sure and steady method God uses to empower you to live in line with your new identity. He makes each day a fresh chance for you to look to Him, the One who's redeemed you, and be "transformed into the same image from glory to glory" (2 Corinthians 3:18). We grow more like Him—more and more—in each season and stage of our lives.

There's actually a word for this process. *Sanctification.* It means to be molded into the image of Jesus. It's how you continue to develop a deeper consistency in your life, a more noticeable similarity to the mind of Christ, to the attitudes of Christ, to the actions of Christ. It doesn't mean your salvation hangs perpetually in the balance while all this is playing out—uncertain and in suspense, as if you just might drop it. No, your salvation is secure forever. But your capacity to experience the many benefits of your salvation will keep expanding "through sanctification by the Spirit" (2 Thessalonians 2:13). Do you see? The Spirit's job is to set up and support the popcorn process in your life.

For the rest of your life.

I hope you're extremely encouraged by this. It means you can count on making progress. Sure, you'll stumble along sometimes. You won't do things perfectly. You'll go home at times realizing you made a big mistake or didn't handle something well. But the Holy Spirit inside you is *with* you for the long haul. The spark of His transforming power is always there to be heated up.

And since God is so excited and invested in showing you (as well as everybody else) what He can reflect of Himself through you, He boils down your responsibility in this process to a basic action that will really get your life sizzling.

All it takes is just *walking.*

> *Do not walk according to the flesh but*
> *according to the Spirit.* (ROMANS 8:4)

He's not asking you to memorize the entire New Testament or attend seminary before He'll start the popping action. He only tells you to start walking. But not the mindless, thoughtless pace of someone who's grown accustomed to walking around in whatever way or direction she pleases. Think of it more like a toddler learning to support her body weight on wobbly little legs.

A young walker who's just starting out doesn't take careless steps. She concentrates fully on what she's doing. The left foot goes . . . *here*. The right foot goes . . . *there*. Each step is diligent and intentional at first. Then pretty soon, the cadence becomes more second nature as she gets used to utilizing those muscles. After a while, over time, it becomes an established, livable habit.

This is what walking by the Spirit looks like.

Throughout your day, as you interact with others and make decisions and choose your actions, pause and carefully consider the step you should take that would most honor God—just as a baby would think carefully about her next step before ever lifting her foot off the ground. Before you make a choice to post that image, or engage in that relationship, or interact with that Twitter conversation, pause and check inwardly to see if your action or attitude reflects your true identity or not. Try determining if it's stemming from an insecurity or fear stirred up by the enemy, or if it's rooted in something real and true. And if you discover, from inside the length of this healthy pause, that you're about to take a step that aligns with lies and not truth, then don't take the step. Instead wait and pray, asking the Holy Spirit to give you courage to take the next step in a way that matches your new identity.

Then . . . walk that way.

It's not always easy, I'll admit, but . . . it's still always basic. It's simple. In fact, if you insist on complicated, I'll give you complicated: Nothing becomes more complicated in a young woman's life than trying to untangle the messes she's made by not being careful about where her feet go. Your choice about taking time to learn how to walk may be wobbly at first, but every minute you invest now will save you many hours down the road, maybe even years, maybe even your life. It'll all be so worth it; I promise you.

So prepare to *cooperate* with God. This is so important. He is a good Father, but even the best parents know they can't do every single thing for their daughter and expect her to grow and mature. There's participation involved. Teamwork. Responsibility. Not because your new life depends entirely on *you,* but because He knows there's nothing more exciting than when you start to see old sins, old barriers, and old obstacles falling down that have kept you from being free for so long. You don't do it all by yourself. You *couldn't* do it all by yourself. But the Spirit lets you play a key part. Together the fire grows hot, the popcorn explodes, the hard shell turns inside out, and you're free to enjoy the delicious result.

Call it sanctification. Call it lasting change.

Call it a delectable difference that enables you to experience God's best for your life.

9

GUILTY AT 65 MPH

I was driving home toward the southern suburbs of Dallas one Saturday afternoon, sailing along I-35 South with the windows cracked open a sliver so the cool fall air could kiss my forehead. Beautiful day. Perfect for cranking up my playlist just a tad and singing along to my favorites as I rolled down the freeway.

The traffic started to thicken as I neared a more congested area, causing me to nudge my left blinker down, meshing seamlessly into the passing lane, trying not to slow my steady pace. I hugged the concrete wall that now lay just outside my driver's side door, separating me from the opposite flow of cars headed north into town. I hadn't touched my brakes in miles, and didn't need to tap them again for as far as the eye could see.

I settled back even more snugly into my seat, sailing past everybody now . . . oblivious to the fact, however, that I'd entered an area where another concrete median had also appeared on the right side of my car. I was humming along in my own exclusive lane, unchallenged by the mere mortals slugging out their afternoon commute on the other side. Except . . .

Wait a minute. Recognition struck. The only vehicles authorized for *this* lane—this special corridor that measured only a single car width—were those with two or more people inside. I'd accidentally drifted into the HOV lane (short for High Occupancy Vehicle), the familiar three-letter symbol that, I now noticed, was boldly painted on both the pavement underneath me and on the signage overhead.

Oh, no.

I was in the wrong spot.

I needed to get out of here.

But I couldn't. The way our interstates are configured in Dallas, you can't just hang a right and weave back into the traffic stream. The HOV lanes continue on for long stretches with openings only every few miles. I was trapped there in the wrong lane.

And to make matters worse, out in the distance between me and the next opportunity to exit was a clearly marked patrol car resting authoritatively on the shoulder.

My heart started flickering fast.

I feel sure now you can probably relate to my dilemma. I don't think I need to telegraph the think-fast conversation I was having with myself in my head. It's like looking up and realizing you're out an hour past curfew, and being pretty sure you're only moments away from a text or phone call that's going to demand some explaining.

I wanted so badly to sail past him and take the chance that the police officer wasn't really watching for lawbreakers at the moment. Maybe he was filling out some paperwork. Maybe he was talking on his radio. Maybe he was munching on a powdered doughnut and not primarily paying attention to the whir of passing cars. Maybe he wouldn't even notice me. One of my kids could technically be slouched down in the back seat. Wasn't true, but . . . could have been. He might just assume it and give me a pass.

(Sigh.) I couldn't risk it, though. Couldn't just keep going. He hadn't yet stepped out and motioned me to pull over. He hadn't flashed his rack lights in choreographed precision with the telltale *WHOOP* on his siren. But I slowed to a stop behind his cruiser anyway, slipped my driver's license from my purse and my official papers from the glove compartment, and shook my disgusted head as I awaited his sauntering, Texas-style, stalking arrival.

When he stepped to the window, asking me what I needed, I pointed around to the inside of the car at my obvious lack of regulation passengers. I admitted I had slid into the HOV lane quite by accident when my mind had wandered on the drive home. I hadn't meant to sneak around traffic illegally. Still, I was in the wrong. I hadn't been paying attention. I was turning myself in. Guilty as not-yet-charged.

This happens in life. We mess up. Sometimes we float into restricted areas. We look up and realize we've veered out of line and need a serious course correction. Or, let's be honest. Sometimes we didn't only get there by accident; we got there on purpose. We knew exactly where the lanes were marked. We knew exactly what all the warning signs were telling us. We weren't in the dark at all about the cost and risk of steering over there—into that kind of attitude or relationship or behavior. We knew exactly what we were doing. We just went ahead and did it anyway. Outright rebellion.

- Like that time we told the lie to cover our tracks;
- Or the time we said yes to the date, even though we already knew the guy's questionable character and morals;

- Or when we spread the rumor, without considering how much it would hurt the other young woman at the other end of the story;
- Or when we went to the party even though we were told outright the kinds of reckless activities planned for the event.

Now we are caught. In the wrong lane.

It's out of step with our identity—to talk like that, to act like that, to behave like that, to think like that—to ignore the Holy Spirit like that. It's inconsistent with who we are. And God, because His goal is not to look for ways to disqualify us but rather to bend us back into the path of blessing, offers us repentance as maybe one of His greatest gifts of all.

Sanctification, as I said, is a major building block toward growing up into your identity. But equally important is the ongoing gift of *repentance*: owning your sin, turning around, getting back on the right road again.

He, more than anyone, knows who we are. "He knows what we are made of, remembering that we are dust" (Psalm 103:14). He knows even though we love Him and worship Him—*we really do!*—our new identity in Christ still shares the living room with old habits that die hard. Sin will always be an option and will always create problems. And make no mistake: He will discipline us like all good fathers do. He does it "for our benefit," the Bible says, "so that we can share his holiness" (Hebrews 12:10), so that we can enjoy "the peaceful fruit of righteousness" (v. 11) reserved for those who respond to His wise choice of correction.

But although the imagery in our heads tells us God is probably fed up with us right now for failing Him again and being in the wrong lane, the words He paints in Scripture tell us something far different. They tell us of One who is "compassionate

and gracious, slow to anger and abounding in faithful love"
(Psalm 103:8), who takes no pleasure in exerting pressure on us
to spin us back the right direction.

That's why throughout the Bible, we see this repeated call
for *returning*—not because God is fed up with *us* but because
we're fed up *ourselves* with what our sin has done to us, especially when He's provided us the salvation, the power, the incen-
tive, the Spirit . . . everything we need for living with "a pure
heart, a good conscience, and a sincere faith" (1 Timothy 1:5).

> *Return to me, for I have redeemed*
> *you.* (ISAIAH 44:22)

> *Return, faithless Israel. . . . I will not look*
> *on you with anger.* (JEREMIAH 3:12)

> *Return, you faithless children. I will heal*
> *your unfaithfulness.* (JEREMIAH 3:22)

> *Take words of repentance with you and*
> *return to the* LORD. (HOSEA 14:2)

> *Return to your God . . . Always put*
> *your hope in God.* (HOSEA 12:6)

Do not, do not, do not stay away—avoiding Him, worried
He's mad about where you've been and what you've done. Do
not feel the need to lie low for a while till His anger dies down.
Do not cover up and hope He'll just let it slide. *Nothing* slides.
He sees *everything.* But when you return to Him in repentance,
you turn your heart toward His light, becoming that prism He
made you to be, where He can beam His eternal love in you.
Then *through* you.

Don't keep going down the wrong lane, little sister.

Pull over.

I braced myself for it. The ticket. The court date. The big fine. The big whine I was already preparing to give my husband that night when I got home and let him know what I'd done.

"You were driving illegally in an HOV lane," the officer said. Sternly. Officially. "That's a violation of state law, punishable as a moving violation."

"Yes, sir. I'm sorry."

"Place your hand right here on the door, ma'am."

I hurriedly cupped it around the slot that held my lowered window.

Creases of smile lines appeared behind his dark sunglasses, even as his lips spread into a manly grin and he let out a small chuckle. "Don't do it again," he said, playfully slapping the back of my hand with his fingertips. "Just be sure you take the next exit up here when you can. Want to get you back on the right road."

And with that, he was off. Back down the shoulder, away from my car, climbing back into his.

The lump in my chest started to melt as I relaxed a bit. I folded up my registration papers and returned them to their place, preparing to resume my trip home. (More carefully this time.) As I drove slowly past the officer's car, I glanced over and meekly waved. *Thank you,* I silently whispered. He gripped the brim of his cap between thumb and forefinger, nodding like a true western lawman.

Repentance complete. Peace restored.

He did it for me. And your heavenly Father is waiting to do it for you.

TO THINK ABOUT

- Which "who you are" or "what you have" statement on page 66 did you find the most inspiring and encouraging to you at this exact moment? Why?
- What is one practical way your identity in Christ has impacted a choice, attitude, or action in your life this week?
- How can you plan to proactively cooperate with the Holy Spirit's work in your life over the next few days—scheduling prayer, spending time in His Word, committing to be obedient to His leading in your life?
- What is one "step" you know you'll have to take this week that you can prepare for right now? How can you plan ahead to walk by the Spirit?

TO TAKE AWAY

As you read your Bible regularly in the days ahead, ask God to show you the realities of what He's done for you and what He continues doing for you—*who you are* and *what you have* because of your relationship with Christ. Write them down. Memorize them. Post them where you can see them often. Repeat them to yourself again and again.

Sanctification is the ongoing process of becoming more and more like Jesus. Be patient with it, persevere in it, and never stop pursuing it.

Repentance is the chance God gives you to turn around from your sins and turn back in the direction He leads you. Never let guilt or shame convince you that the Father won't receive you. His grace is sufficient. His mercy is everlasting.

PART THREE

WALK IN THE LIGHT

Read This

You have put off the old self with its practices and have put on the new self. You are being renewed in knowledge according to the image of your Creator. (COLOSSIANS 3:9–10)

Say This

My struggles do not define me. Just because I've done something or have felt something doesn't mean that's who I am. My identity is rooted in my new nature in Christ. So I will be vigilant and proactive in standing firm against the enemy's attempts to steal my peace, joy, and contentment. I will be a woman of integrity who institutes healthy boundaries that let me honor my God-given identity. I will guard my spiritual treasures by choosing my friends carefully, learning from godly mentors, and walking in a manner worthy of God's calling on my life.

Believe This

If we walk in the light as he himself is in the light, we have fellowship with one another, and the blood of Jesus his Son cleanses us from all sin. (1 JOHN 1:7)

10

TUG-OF-WAR

Every summer of my childhood, I spent at least a week, sometimes two, at Pine Cove Christian Camp. It was eventful for
many reasons, but one of the highlights each year was the epic
tug-of-war match. Two dozen people would scamper toward
either end of a long, thick rope, grasping its broad circumference
with both hands and readying themselves to pull.

The stakes were high. The losers would fall face-first into the
gargantuan, man-made mud puddle that loomed in between.

So we corkscrewed our feet into the ground, anchoring the
full weight of our bodies into a solid foothold. We widened our
stances, bending ourselves into a sturdy crouch, lowering our center of gravity. And we waited . . . waited for the person in charge to
blow that whistle, even as we tensed our muscles in preparation.

Ready?

READY!!!

The whistle blew. Fierce battle ensued. Pulling, bracing, leaning, screaming—whatever it took. Because we knew. We knew
what losing meant. We knew if we let up for even a second, the
momentum we could feel already building from the other side

would yank us so far off balance that we'd never be able to recover . . . which of course would lead to a predictable end. Wet. Messy. Disgusting. Muddy.

War. Tug-of-war. Don't you feel it? Every day?

Even when you're doing nothing to invite it or incite it, you'll often feel the tug from the other end of your life's rope—the tug of sin, the tug of temptation, the tug of a very real enemy— seeking to muddy your soul and body. It can feel stronger at some times than at others. At first it may be only a little twitch, barely enough to notice, just enough to bother you with an enticing temptation. But pretty soon it's really pressing. Pressuring you. Fighting against you. Swaying you. Pulling hard. Pulling harder. You don't know if you can hold out much longer.

You want to live for Christ. You know what's right. You know what your best days as a believer have all been like. But today, at this moment, you feel the tug. Drawing you to give in to a fleshly passion. Teasing you toward an unruly ambition. Pumping you full of doubts and lies. Then—the moment you start thinking they're true and you stop pulling against their momentum—they drag you into the mud, where the tug always leads when you haven't taken it seriously and fortified yourself against it.

This spiritual tug-of-war is not unique to you. It's a reality shared by the entire human population. Even one of the most incredible Christians who ever lived said he felt and dealt with the same thing. Paul the apostle, who wrote nearly half the books in the New Testament, described his struggle like this:

*I don't really understand myself, for I want
to do what is right, but I don't do it. Instead, I
do what I hate. . . . I want to do what is good,
but I don't. I don't want to do what is wrong,
but I do it anyway. But if I do what I don't
want to do, I am not really the one doing
wrong; it is sin living in me that does it.*

*I have discovered this principle of life—that
when I want to do what is right, I inevitably
do what is wrong. I love God's law with all
my heart. But there is another power within
me that is at war with my mind. This power
makes me a slave to the sin that is still within
me. Oh, what a miserable person I am! Who
will free me from this life that is dominated
by sin and death?* (ROMANS 7:15, 18-24 NLT)

Can't you hear the angst and sadness in his voice? The fact that his heart and flesh could cave so easily bothered him. The fact that he didn't always maintain the motivation and muscle tone to keep himself out of the mud drove him crazy. *"I don't really understand myself"*—just like we often don't really understand ourselves either. Despite knowing about the mud, the mess, and the mound of dirty laundry waiting on the other end of that rope, Paul still didn't always tug back. And neither do we.

During college, for instance, I didn't tug as much as I should have. Almost immediately after arriving on campus, I got caught up in a slew of relationships and activities that were clearly not in my best interest. I knew I shouldn't be allowing myself to draw so closely to those influences, those places, and those people. But despite my authentic internal desire, I kept caving—participating, indulging, allowing. Then I'd go to class the next day, all muddied with the grime of guilt and self-reproach because, like Paul, *I did not understand* why I kept letting myself get into this mess again and again.

The battle is just so real for all of us.

But the worst feeling in the world is knowing that this forbidden thing you believe you need—whatever that thing may be—is likely going to cause you pain and loss, and yet you still want it anyway. What a struggle.

It's everyone's struggle.

. . . .

I've mentioned already that our struggle with sin goes back to the garden of Eden. Our first parents sinned. They bore sinful children. And all the people who spring from their family tree—which would be every single one of us—have each been born with a heart that leans toward sin. The struggle is ingrained. The struggle is universal.

But the struggle is also personal.

Let me map it out for you.

Think of your sin nature as being like the Mississippi River, which runs more than two thousand miles, crossing into ten states, until it ultimately empties into the Gulf of Mexico. Each of our lives has been tainted by one main trunk line of sin like that. One big reservoir. It pours through all of us, swirls all around us, picks us up off our feet, and takes us steadily downstream. But at the place where the mighty Mississippi starts leveling out, down around southern Louisiana, it branches off into little fingers, called *distributaries.* It fans out into what's called a "bird foot" pattern. This one huge river becomes hundreds of individual veins of water.

Sin is like that too. It's like one big pool that divides into rivulets, expressing itself uniquely in individuals. It shows up differently in you than in me. Like a delta breaking off into distributaries, the original rush of sin that permeates all of our lives takes up its own expression in every different person.

That's because Satan, aware of each of our specific personalities (the interests, desires, experiences, and passions God has placed in us), takes advantage of what he knows about us. These predispositions are not sinful in themselves. But he can match them up with temptations that strike closer to our own hearts than they might to someone else's. And if he catches us at the wrong time, he might be able to turn those tendencies and temperaments against us, into sinful leanings that are specific to us.

So, while one person may struggle with substance abuse, another may struggle with telling the truth. One may be prone to cheating or stealing, while another may go to extremes in her intake of food. A girl over here may be having a terrible time controlling her anger, unwilling to forgive, even as a girl walking right past her—poisoned by the same pool of original sin—finds her biggest battle in keeping herself pure from sexual sin.

Same river; different distributaries.

Same source; different expressions.

Same struggle; different people.

Please, please, please hear me clearly when I tell you that I'm about to say. I know you struggle; and I want you to know that I struggle too. Each one of us knows the particular temptations that yank the hardest on our own attempts at standing strong and steady for Christ. Yours and mine may be somewhat the same, or they may be dramatically different. But either way . . .

You are *not* your *struggle*.

Your *struggle* is *not* your *identity*.

Your Struggle ≠ Your Identity

I meet so many people today—your age and older—who berate themselves severely, not only because of their sin, but simply because they're *struggling* against sin. They interpret the mere battle itself—whether it's against a pattern of thinking or behaving or feeling or whatever—as a sign of failure, even a lack of salvation, as if the struggle alone confirms who they are.

We all have these leanings toward particular desires, and we all must determine to pull back against them throughout our lives. If we don't, if we slip into neutral, they'll drag us down. But still, these tendencies don't define us. They're just the war zone where we struggle.

And there's a difference.

My heart breaks when I see a person internalize a label based on a struggle he or she is wrestling with. A young boy who has feminine tendencies, for example, or a young girl who experiences attraction to another female and is labeled as "gay." And so, they believe they must be. Because that's what they've been told they are, simply because that's where they struggle.

Another young person struggles through a season of sexual sin, or stumbles home after drinking too much at a college party. And she's berated, told she'll never change, that she's destined to be just like one of her parents who ended up being irresponsible, unfaithful, and crippled by addiction. So she starts to live up to it. Or, should I say, live down to it. Young people like this believe they must be the thing they're struggling with. The line between *who they are* and *what they've done* or *what they've struggled with* or *how they feel* becomes quickly blurred.

It's crucial, as you navigate the days and weeks of your life, that you separate your struggle from your identity as Paul did. In the same book where he bravely exposed his failures and faults, he testifies of his status as *called* and *set apart*

(Romans 1:1), *freed* from the curse of sin (6:18), *unburdened* by condemnation (8:1), a *child of God* and *co-heir* with Christ Jesus (8:16–17) and . . . a victorious *overcomer* (8:37).

This is who He was.

This is who you are.

You may have done something, you may feel something, you may have experienced something, but it doesn't mean you *are* that something. You are who *God* says you are. Point-blank. Period. Your name and labels are what God's Word declares about you.

I'll say it again: you are who *God* says you are. And not even your most intensive point of struggle can reconfigure the person He's made you to be.

Feel the tug? Sure. Of course you do. We all do. Each one of us feels it in our own specific, personalized way. But don't let it guilt you or shame you or compel you to live in a way that doesn't line up with the truth. Don't allow someone to discourage you by implying you've done something wrong merely because you find it hard not to feel drawn toward this, that, or whatever.

This means war. But don't cave.

With all your might, and by the power of God's Spirit . . . *pull!*

11

GUARDED TREASURES

Following my senior year in high school, my parents gave me a trip to London as a graduation gift—not because we were so rich and lavish, but because my aunt Ruth lived there (which meant I had a free place to stay), and my parents knew she'd keep an eye on me and the friend they said could come along with me.

You'd think, having a full week to explore London, we'd want to visit the most historic, iconic sites and tour the royal residences. But we didn't want to do the touristy, tour-guided things. We just wanted to walk the streets aimlessly for hours at a time, ducking into little boutiques and candy shops whenever something appealed to us.

One day we caught the bus near my aunt's house and went to see a movie at a little theater in Piccadilly Circus. Afterward we walked to a doughnut shop across the street and ordered our favorite chocolate-filled, sugar-glazed treats. The guy behind the counter told me how much my order would cost, and I fished inside my purse for the right amount. But my money . . . it was *gone!* . . . all the dollars we'd exchanged for British pounds earlier in the day.

Seeing my panicked expression, and feeling the line form-ing impatiently behind us, my friend stepped around me and offered to pay for both of us. But as she reached into her own wallet, she too made the same shocking discovery. *Both* of us had lost our money.

We'd been robbed!

But where? How? No idea. Not until we'd walked out of the store shame-faced and back to the movie theater did we begin to figure it out. The manager told us that a string of thieves had recently been targeting tourists. Apparently, our thief inten-tionally sat behind us in the theater and slid our purses silently back to him from around our feet. Then, to buy himself time, he put our wallets back inside each purse after removing all their money, and then returned them to the place where he'd found them. Genius. He knew we'd be halfway home before we even noticed anything was missing.

If only we'd kept our bags in our laps, not on the floor.

If only we'd kept them under our control at all times.

If so, we could've had our movie, and had our doughnuts, and still had our money and memories to enjoy at the end. We could've had *all* the good things—just the way we intended—if only we'd been more proactive, more intentional, about guard-ing something that was valuable and important.

. . . .

Your life, your time, your heart, your sense of identity—each of these forms of personal currency is precious. And guarding them must be a top priority. They demand serious, diligent commitments to their proper care and keeping. If you leave their safety to chance without a plan, assuming they'll probably be okay—if you choose not to put much thought into protecting and honoring your God-given treasures—you'll look down one day and find that they're gone.

And you'll have no idea where you lost them.

The enemy is too sly and smart just to come up and try to snatch spiritual valuables right out of your hand, in front of your face. You'd know you'd been robbed then. You'd call the police. You'd give descriptions. You'd work to get them back if you could.

Instead Satan sneaks them out the back door, slipping them out from under your feet, sliding them away from you in small quantities, just enough where you won't even notice they're missing . . . until you're completely empty handed and realize you've been shafted. Through the squandering of an hour *here*, or the small compromise of a conviction *there*, the meter starts running until it's quietly rung up a costly bill. Then, like my friend and me at the London sweet shop, you're suddenly not free to do the things you ought to be able to enjoy . . . because you weren't careful enough, weren't intentional enough, to keep your most valuable things protected, to *keep your hand on that spiritual purse at all times* instead of being lulled to sleep, hypnotized by the entertaining distractions swirling around you.

I don't want him stealing from you like that, little sis.

One of the places where you're often in danger of being robbed in this way is through social media. If you aren't careful and measured in your intake of content and online conversation, the things you absorb can slowly break apart your confidence and identity. With social media, you're constantly being inundated with images and ideas that can so easily shape the way you think, can change the way you feel about yourself, and can adjust the parameters on how you relate to the world around you.

It's true, the plusses and benefits of modern technologies are astounding. Being able to express yourself. Quickly finding out what's going on in the world and with people you know. Keeping up with your friends. Communicating with family and others who live in different parts of the country, even different parts of the world. Social media is staggering. It's powerful. As a woman in ministry, I'm grateful all the time for how it allows me to speak so widely and quickly and easily with people . . . and even better, how it allows me to hear back from them.

I love it just like you love it.

But we all need to be careful that we don't love it more than we love having peace of mind. Or more than being content with who we are and with what God has given us. Or more than spending time with Him and letting His Word speak truth to us. Or more than being absolutely sure of what really matters in life—our family, our priorities, and our God-given purpose.

I don't want to lose *any* of that. Do you?

That's why I want to encourage you to be proactive when it comes to guarding your heart and mind. I'm convinced that just as easily as the screen in that London theater distracted me from guarding my purse, the screen in your hand can distract you from guarding yours. All day every day, it calls to you, enticing you to engage without concern for how it may be affecting your emotional, spiritual, and even physical health. Or simply whittling away at your precious time. All the while, the enemy creeps by, ready to rob the unsuspecting.

The power of social media to distort our identity mostly comes not from the fact that we're using it at all, but simply from the fact that we use it *all the time,* leaving other more important things unattended while we do. The messages and images we're constantly consuming twist our sense of worth, making us feel insecure or lonely or discontented. The mocking voice of comparison and competition grows steadily louder and louder, until the trusted voice of God is dulled to a whisper. We start longing for things we actually already have in Him, like peace, acceptance, and freedom. We begin to hunger and obsess about the attention and approval we do or don't receive there, instead of standing steady in the approval that God has already given us and will *always* give us. We start trying to become something we're not, in hopes of impressing people we don't even really know.

One young lady in my life described the impact that unrestricted access to social media was having on her heart:

> *The energy it was taking to want things I didn't have, that I was never meant to have, was crippling . . . and expensive. I've decided it's cheaper to just be myself. In the past, I longed to be like the Instagram girls I saw who were ROCKIN' IT! From being stylish to having the perfect home, there was a gang of beautiful and talented young women out there, and I wanted a piece of their lives. But I had to learn that what's for them is for them, and what's for me is for me. When I stopped worrying about trying to be like them, the weight was lifted. Insta-stalking, NO MORE!*

Here's a girl who decided to get a firm grip again on her treasures and no longer leave them to the enemy's disposal. And just as you can, she discovered a God-given blessing to help with that.

Boundaries.

The self-discipline of boundaries is a gift God makes available to you, not to frustrate or confine you, but to help you be truly satisfied with all the things He's given. When you set boundaries, you can keep enjoying those things without them becoming more important to you than He is. Setting boundaries—making *margin*—helps you deal with all kinds of joy thieves that are lurking around your twenty-first-century life, even though it's a concept that actually predates social media by at least four thousand years.

When the children of Israel were freed from four hundred years of captivity in Egypt, they began an eighteen-month journey toward their new home in the promised land. Along the way, the Lord gave them many memorable gifts, including "manna" (Exodus 16:31)—Frosted Flakes from heaven. These Israelites were out in the middle of nowhere, and God chose to provide them with this deliciously filling form of food that somehow fell from heaven overnight so that it was there on the ground to meet them when they woke up every morning.

The word *manna*, by the way, means . . . "Wha-a-a-t?" I'm serious. When the Israelites first saw it, they said to one another, "What is it?" (Exodus 16:15). Like, *this is so cool!* Every morning it was like a brand-new miracle.

But like anything good and desirable, too much of it can become like a little god in your life. Instead of keeping your heart focused on God, who the Bible says "richly provides us with all things to enjoy" (1 Timothy 6:17), you can easily start loving the food instead of loving Him and His truth. Easy for that kind of switch to happen.

Which is why, to keep this from happening to the Israelites, God gave them another gift along with the food He was feeding them. A secret ingredient, called . . .

"Sabbath."

Here's how it worked. God told the people they could pop out of their tents, every day of the week, and gather up as much manna as they needed for that day. They were supposed to restrain themselves from gathering more than needed for the day stretched out in front of them. And then, on the seventh day—the Sabbath day—He told them to rest, not to go out foraging. And He made them a promise. He said He'd make sure the amount of manna they brought inside with them on the sixth day would be plenty to tide them over through the weekend. They could have both their manna *and* their rest. Best of both worlds. Refusing to overindulge by trusting God for their daily bread and implementing Sabbath margin—the Sabbath boundary—was not a restriction but a gift. It helped them to keep depending on their God, enjoying their freedom instead of lapsing into fear and discontentment.

Because guess what happens if you accept the manna without the margin? Those who insisted on doing it their own strong-willed way and who went out to gather manna on the day they should have been resting found nothing on the Sabbath to satisfy their hunger. The wilderness ground was covered only with the sand they walked on. What a waste of time. And, during the weekdays, anyone who hoarded more manna than a daily allotment found that their leftovers became spoiled and foul. Stinky and hard to live with.

This is exactly what happens when we start consuming too much of something—anything—without boundaries, without margin, without responsibility, without a Sabbath mentality. Instead of being a helpful, enjoyable gift, we either begin to feel frustrated and exhausted because we can no longer find what we are searching for, or it becomes something that sickens us and makes us unhealthy. Instead of being a gift that we use at a reasonable pace, freely enjoying its fun and benefits, "the gift" starts ferociously taking us over, turning itself into a compulsion. It permeates a foulness in our lives—an anxiety and worry that wafts through our hearts and minds. Now we are controlled by it, enslaved to it—hungrier than ever for it, despite the fact that we've already been gobbling down way too much of it.

Think of the media you're consuming. Is it starting to consume you? Does it make you feel peaceful and joy-filled? Are you even having fun anymore? Or is it making you feel worse? Riddled with anxiety and worry? Constantly comparing yourself? Belittling yourself? Feeling bad about yourself? Do jealousy and envy build in your heart and then catch like wildfire until they have burned down whatever was left of your sense of significance and joy? Are you starting to look around at your own life, at yourself, with disgust?

If you've noticed this pattern, and if it's occupying too much of your thoughts, begin placing some healthy margin and boundaries around it. Choose times when you will deliberately step away from your phone, your tablet, or your computer and not engage in social media activity for an *hour* here or there—for a *day* here or there—not allowing it to become an uncontrollable obsession that takes your eyes off your treasures.

Because consider this: the Israelites had been slaves in Egypt for so long that they couldn't even grasp the concept of Sabbath at first. Their lives had always been seven days a week, nonstop, do more, do it now. That's what an enslaved life looks like. They weren't in control of their time or their schedule. They never received any break from the commands of their taskmasters who imposed brutal demands on them. And maybe you've felt this way a lot in terms of your screen time, as if you're required to keep it up, that you can't afford to go without it.

That's what a slave mentality is like.

But a Sabbath mentality frees you from that. It reminds you that you don't have to be bossed around like that.

Margin is a *gift*. Boundaries are God's gift to you. The Israelites didn't lose anything by backing away from their manna collecting for a day. In fact, they actually accumulated something more—time to spend with the One who made them and provided for them and affirmed their intrinsic, incomparable worth as His children.

So while it would be easy for someone like me to sit here picking apart the dangers and pitfalls of social media—and there are lots of them, of course—I believe there's generally less need to go cold turkey in abstaining from it than to learn how to better manage it. Because when God gives us things to use and enjoy, He gives them along with proper ways of handling them so that we can *truly* enjoy them, *freely* enjoy them.

And never be robbed by them.

12

SECURING YOUR PERIMETER

Near the end of my first semester at college, one of my dearest, lifelong friends came to visit. Jada and I hadn't seen each other in months, and we started our weekend of fun by—what else?—shopping! We went from one store to another in quick succession, just grabbing clothes off the rack, darting in and out of dressing rooms, and then laughing or commenting on each other's choices.

At one point, I came out wearing a mid-thigh skirt and pranced over to the mirror while Jada stood behind me, noticeably silent. "What? You don't like it?" I asked—checking myself out, glancing back at her, trying to interpret this mysterious look she was giving me.

(Wait for it, wait for it, wait for it.)

"Pri-SCILL-a!" she finally blurted out, as if seeing me poured into this tiny mini skirt had made it too hard for her to contain herself any longer. "Girl, that skirt is way too short! Your mom would *never* let you wear that! And you probably shouldn't let you wear it either."

Well . . .

She was right. There in that mirror, I *saw* the skirt. I'd looked at it in the dressing room before coming out to show her, but I didn't see it clearly until my friend's honesty opened up my eyes.

We all need honest, loving friends like that—the kind who will reach around and fix your collar if it's standing up weird in the back—the kind who will tell you when you've got a little sprig of lunch stuck between your teeth—the kind who care more about *you* than about how you feel about *them*. They tell you the truth. They shoot you straight.

Because they love you. For real.

The trouble with being your own independent navigator for how you should walk is that you'll inevitably form blind spots. Even with long camera rolls of selfies on your phone and more ways than ever before to help you see yourself in 360-degree perspective, you can still be convinced that an attitude you're taking, or a decision you're considering, or a flirtation with compromise that you've decided to entertain is probably not so big of a deal, that it's a healthy move for you.

But what if it's unhealthy and toxic and problematic, except you can't see it? What if it's riskier and more rebellious than you think? What if it's going to cost you more in the end than you ever thought you'd have to pay? Maybe to another person's more careful eye, this same decision that seems so tame and innocent to you has warning signs flashing and blaring all over it. But because it's something you want to do, and because you've not really asked anybody to weigh in on it who'd be more inclined to disagree with you, you're trudging ahead without anyone to break your fall.

Sometimes, in life's tug-of-war, you're about to fall in the mud, but you don't know it.

That's why *accountability* matters—maintaining at least a small nucleus of faithful, healthy, God-honoring friends who will talk with you about things and pray about things and point out things. Accountability is a vital, protective add-on to your life, throughout *all* your life.

But more than seeking out these kinds of good influences among girls your own age, you also need something else if you want to be covered left and right, on all sides, from the distortions you might be tempted to believe. You need *mentors* who've already walked the road ahead of you with integrity and character, people who have hindsight on their side. You need some women from whom you can receive insight about where you are, what you're doing, and how it all lines up with who God has created you to be.

I was reminded of this valuable truth on an exciting trip I made a number of years ago to India. One of the highlights of being there—if you don't count getting to enjoy those yummy loaves of flatbread called *naan*—was being able to wear an authentic suit of traditional Indian clothing while speaking to a group of local women.

In case you didn't know, in India women wear a garment called a *sari* (pronounced like the "sorry" you might say to your brother after nabbing the last piece of naan, for example). They handcrafted a beautiful gown for me, made of delectable fabrics in a bright green color trimmed with gold accents. But to my Texas American style, it didn't look like a dress at all. There weren't any holes for my head and arms, no tidy little zipper in the back. Instead it hung in loose waves of flat material. How was I supposed to put this thing on?

Turns out, putting on a sari requires a precise wrapping process mastered by the women of India, and they were eager to show me how it's done. So while I dutifully removed my jeans and T-shirt, a kind Indian woman wrapped the sari intricately around my body, using large pins to secure it in strategic gatherings, before finishing it all off with one last drape that cascaded elegantly over my shoulder.

Gorgeous? Yes.

Easy to walk in? No . . . not to the untrained.

So I left my hotel that evening feeling as though I'd been stuffed inside a burrito. But that's okay, this same lovely woman told me. She'd be close beside me, she said, all night long to help me manage it.

I wasn't sure how I felt about this arrangement at first—having someone trailing with me, fussing with the fit of my clothes the whole evening. Watching me go up and down stairs and even (ahem) going into the bathroom with me? Yes, she even went in *there* with me.

But I quickly realized that I couldn't make it without her. I would have never have been able to put those gazillions of perfectly placed pins back in position and walk back out in public decently. I *needed* a woman like her—someone with her experience, with her dedication, with her time, and with her willingness to share. I had so much to gain from being around someone whose firsthand lifetime of knowledge navigating these clothes could compensate for the obvious gaps in what I was equipped to figure out on my own, on the fly.

What a blessing that dear woman became to me—the same blessings that I guarantee you'll experience by intentionally positioning yourself around a wiser, more experienced woman than you—someone to walk beside you regularly, routinely, or even just every so often on your journey. As you "take off your former way of life, the old self"—and as you learn how to "be renewed in the spirit of your minds, and to put on the new self, the one created according to God's likeness in righteousness and purity of the truth" (Ephesians 4:22-24)—you'll need someone to come alongside who knows a thing or two about walking in these new clothes.

Whether it's your mom or a grandmother, a godly relative, or someone in your church, school, or neighborhood, be on the lookout for women who've walked the road a little bit longer than you, and who've successfully worn the spiritual clothes you're trying to put on now. In fact, make it a matter of prayer. Ask the Lord to open your eyes to the sincere believers who may already be present in your life—even distantly—who would love investing in you and letting you learn from their successes and failures.

I'll admit to you: I didn't really appreciate the value of a mentor's guidance when I was a teenager. I was sure I could take care of myself just fine without anyone else's help. I was too full of myself to even notice such people were out there. But I missed out on something I needed. Believing you don't need the wisdom of older women in your life is a crazy lie—a lie of pride, a lie of unrealistic expectations, a lie of disrespect for others, not to mention a lie of irresponsibility toward those who could benefit from your sweet presence in their lives as well.

So, if I could go back and tell my younger self a truth she really needed to hear, I'd tell her something that I thankfully, eventually, much later, finally came around to understanding, same as I'm telling you here today. Prayerfully and intentionally share your life with other women who can serve as mentors to you. I'm confident you'll find, as I did—and still do—the importance of and security that comes from having someone nearby to show you how to wear your new identity well.

TO THINK ABOUT

- What are your struggles? In what ways have you been mistaking your struggle for your identity?
- How can you stand guard against the enemy's scheme for taking advantage of you through these areas of life where you struggle?
- What kinds of emotions do you generally feel when engaged on social media? What kinds of modifications and boundaries can you put in place to take control of this part of your life? Who should you unfollow? What margin can you proactively build in?
- Who is one or more persons your age who you could benefit from spending more time around? Who's an older woman you could ask about becoming your mentor?

TO TAKE AWAY

Social media can be fun, entertaining, and informative, but it can also infuse steady doses of doubt and discouragement about your identity. Take the initiative yourself to impose limits. Construct boundaries around your social media use. Consider taking a day or a week off every month, spending those hours engaging with real life and real people, letting God's voice feed your self-worth. See if you feel better about who He's made you to be.

If your friends fuel your insecurity rather than help you rest in God's purposes for your life, you should instead find a group of people who value living in truth, in helping each other to be authentic and honor God. Be sure you're routinely around people with whom you can be yourself, not needing to impress them or be someone you're not.

PART FOUR

LIGHT OF THE WORLD

Read This

*You were once darkness, but now you are
light in the Lord. Live as children of light—for
the fruit of the light consists of all goodness,
righteousness, and truth.* (EPHESIANS 5:8–9)

Say This

God has given me a mission. A supernatural
assignment. He has placed me here in this time, in
this place, in my generation, to perform tasks that
require someone just like me to complete them.
Even my weaknesses and shortcomings are part
of what He'll use to do His work through me. My
mission starts now, today, by being faithful and
obedient to everything He puts before me. This
is His will for me. Simply to follow Him.

Believe This

*You are the light of the world. A city situated on a
hill cannot be hidden. . . .
Let your light shine before others, so that they
may see your good works and give glory to
your Father in heaven.* (MATTHEW 5:14, 16)

13

NOW SERVING:
YOUR GENERATION

No one is completely positive of the exact date when David was born—the kid who would one day be king of Israel. But there's general agreement that he was around sixteen when Samuel (the man who basically functioned as the people's chief authority and spiritual conscience) informed him that God had chosen David for this lofty position.

> *The Lord said, "Anoint him, for he is the one."*
> *So Samuel took the horn of oil and anointed*
> *him in the presence of his brothers, and the*
> *Spirit of the Lord came powerfully on David*
> *from that day forward.* (1 SAMUEL 16:12-13)

Here's the catch, though. Israel already *had* a king: King Saul. True, he was a scamp, a pretender. He was tall and good-looking on the outside, but spindly and spineless on the inside. And yet for the time being—and nobody else but God knew how long that time would be—Saul was the guy who was wearing the crown.

So try putting yourself in David's shoes for a minute. He's a teenager. He's a nobody. He's the kid brother in a large family of strapping, rugged males. Not even his own father, Jesse, thought he was worth rustling out of the sheep pasture when Samuel, the great judge and leader, passed through town to meet Jesse and his sons. Still, at God's command, after determining that none of these young men were king material, Samuel told Jesse to go get David out of the sheepfold, because he was the one the Lord had chosen.

After this encounter with Samuel, David knew his future contained a significant increase in power, position, and pay grade. David's life was on an upward trajectory and headed someplace really special, with the opportunity to make a real impact on the world. Isn't that what we all want? To matter? To make a difference? To give our lives to something bigger? Though hard to believe, David's future was guaranteed—money in the bank—simply waiting out there for him to grow up a bit, and then the crown would be his. God had promised. Can't get any more certain than that.

But despite this unexpected little ceremony where Samuel declared him king, David's next move—are you ready for this?—was to go back and see how his sheep were doing. Fathom that. Being anointed as king of Israel had just been his lunch break that day. In fact, for the next twelve or thirteen years, David cycled through a number of different job descriptions on his way to becoming king. Some of them were mundane and underwhelming—like delivering cheese to his brothers on the battlefield. Others were a bit more prestigious, more notable, more challenging—like being a giant killer and slaying a nine-foot champion named Goliath. Other positions ran the gamut from musician to armor-bearer.

What I'm saying is: David's divine mission wasn't just about the throne. It also included all the other tasks he took on and tackled before he ever wore a crown. The assignment God had given him started immediately—at sixteen years old, in a field, watching over smelly sheep. God's will looked like *this.* It looked like *today,* not waiting on a crown to materialize tomorrow. David's mission throughout his life, even as a teenager, was to serve God diligently wherever he found himself next. As Acts 13:36 says it, David's life was summarized by "serving God's purpose in his own generation."

In other words, he wasn't dependent on being king before he could feel like he was doing something of kingdom importance. No matter the task before him, at any point along the way, he saw it as a meaningful contribution, a way of serving God with the part of his life that he was currently living. His mission was always the same, despite whatever job he was doing at the time.

So watch this:

- When he was tending sheep, he was serving the purposes of God.
- When he was delivering cheese, he was serving the purposes of God.
- When he was playing music, he was serving the purposes of God.
- When he was slaying a giant, he was serving the purposes of God.

It all stayed in line for him. Because his goal never changed. This was his mission. To serve God. In every time and place.

Your mission is the same as well—to serve God in your time and place, to serve His purposes in your generation. At the end of your life, you want to be able to look back and say you did what God put you here to do, the way He wanted you to do it. And the time and place to start doing it is now.

What are you waiting on? A crown?

Girl, you're already wearing it. So get busy living it!

In your season of life today, perhaps you're a student, a single young woman. You're a daughter and a friend. You may also be a sister, a techie, a blogger, a musician, an athlete, an artist, a leader. As the years unfold, the seasons of your life will change, and you'll become your own unique combination of possibilities: maybe a business owner, wife, mother, world traveler, a woman in ministry, a hardworking employee or freelancer in one or more fields. You'll fill different roles and responsibilities specific to you. Some will be dull and humdrum, but others will feel like fireworks exploding in your heart. But during each time frame, within each context, your commitment to the mission should be the same as David's. Serving the purposes of God. Wherever you are. Whatever you're doing. In *your* generation. In *this* generation.

Because your mission starts now.

And right now, your life today is how it looks.

But here's what's so cool about what we learn from watching David's life:

> He [God] chose David, his servant, handpicked
> him from his work in the sheep pens. One day
> he was caring for the ewes and their lambs, the
> next day God had him shepherding Jacob, his
> people Israel, his prize possession. His good
> heart made him a good shepherd; he guided the
> people wisely and well. (PSALM 78:70-72 MSG)

From shepherd to king. It was all connected.

Do you see it?—the sturdy bridge between what David was doing when we first meet him (tending sheep) and what he eventually grew up to do and become (ruling a nation). Many of the skills he learned as a lowly shepherd were both direct and indirect preparation for his role of being king.

David couldn't have recognized this, of course, while he was herding sheep for hours on end. And listen to me: neither will you. Today's task can often seem like such a waste of time, as if it has absolutely no bearing on what you believe God has in mind for you, on what you see yourself becoming. You may even be thinking about quitting. This stuff is just not what you want to be doing right now. But David didn't disengage from even the most menial task. He invested himself as a young person into a flock of mindless sheep. He tenderly helped them find food and good grazing land. He fiercely fended off intruders and attackers, protecting the animals entrusted to his care.

And good thing he did, because he'd need some of those same skills when he traded his sheep for a nation full of people. They too needed to be guided, guarded, and protected by an able leader. They too needed a selfless, servant-hearted person who would put their collective interests and safety above his own. If he hadn't thrown all of himself into those long, boring days under a hot Middle Eastern sun, he wouldn't have been ready when the time came for him to step even more fully into his generation and show them what God could do through a person who'd made his life a long habit of serving Him.

Many strands of connective tissue exist between your *now* and the *later* version of your mission to your generation. The things you'll be doing *then* are already in the process of being pieced together and practiced and cultivated today.

It's already your turn.

It's already your time.

The crown is already on your head. Your divine mission is significantly and intricately tied to what you're doing right now.

Don't miss it because you're anxiously looking ahead, discontented with the things God has given you today.

The opportunity to honor God with your life is already in your hand.

Whatever He has asked you to do today, do it with all your heart.

14

"HOW CAN I KNOW GOD'S WILL?"

et's get personal now. Let's connect David's story to yours. And mine. Let's gather up what we've been discovering about identity and begin making some links between *who we are* and *what we do*.

I can't tell you how many times I'm asked a version of the following question by young women like you:

How can I know God's will for my life?

It's a good question. An important question. I've asked it of myself quite often throughout the years. (Still do sometimes.)

In high school, I wanted to have certainty about what my college major should be. No flexibility. I wanted to make an exact decision and have all my plans in place. I was also anxious that I'd never find the right guy to have a real grown-up relationship with.

In college, I was a single woman who interned as a part-time radio disc jockey. I spent too much of my time and energy worried about when/if my career path would ever line up with my original ambition to pursue broadcast journalism. And I longed to be in a committed relationship, headed toward marriage.

When would I ever get to God's will for my life?

In my early twenties, I became a graduate student and landed a few short-lived opportunities in television. I also started leading a Bible study for ten female students. Yet I was in a rush to hurry through school. I never wanted to write another paper again. I was just eager to get started on a full-time career, wondering what God had planned for me next. To top it off, I had a broken heart after a bad breakup with a longtime boyfriend. I felt dejected, discouraged, and delayed in getting started at being an adult.

When would I ever get to God's will for my life?

At twenty-four, I married a wonderful man and started my life as a newlywed wife. My work, however, wasn't going so wonderfully. Disappointed because the doors of television still seemed closed to me, I fell back on a plan B option, taking a job as a speaker for corporate groups in business settings. I felt a lot of discouragement and insecurity because of how my desired career path had failed to pan out. I still taught the women's Bible study, but fewer than ten students came now. Was I doing what God had planned for me? Was this it?

When would I ever get to God's will for my life?

In my late twenties and early thirties, I began to sense God leading me into full-time ministry, right as my family was starting to grow. I was soon mothering small babies and seeking to share God's Word whenever the opportunity arrived. I was officially unemployed. And overwhelmed. Why was He birthing this fresh desire in me, just as I was having babies—to whom I was thrilled to give the best of my time and attention?

How could I best honor God's will for my life?

Sometime in my thirties, a publisher invited me to put a particular message I'd been teaching into the format of a video-driven Bible study—writing it, filming it. I questioned my ability to navigate a project like that since I'd never done anything like it before. I found myself battling again with that same old insecurity and fear. Would this project fail like my local Bible study seemingly had? Like my TV career had? Maybe I was just juggling a few too many things at once—marriage, mothering, ministry. It was a fast pace.

Was this God's will for my life?

I know you're wondering it too.

Should I try out for that team? Should I make a time commitment to that volunteer organization? Should I date this guy? Should I take a job this summer? Should I choose that college? Should I say no to that opportunity? I've just got so many decisions to make, and I don't know what to do . . .

How can I know God's will?

I'm totally confident that you're pondering this question from an honorable desire to please Him. The mere fact that you're asking it means you realize He's put you on this earth for a reason, for a plan, and you genuinely want to live out His purposes for your life with your time and your God-given talents. You want to be exactly where you're supposed to be, doing exactly what you're supposed to be doing. And that's obviously a good place to have your heart. I'd much rather hear you asking this question than not caring enough to think about it at all.

But usually, when we ask it, we're hoping for a concrete, nuts-and-bolts, thoroughly mapped out, here's-your-answer response that gives us undeniable proof we're doing precisely what God wants. Right now. We want something definite. Times and dates. GPS coordinates. Written details and instructions.

But listen carefully: often it's the *journey itself* that is God's will. He's taking you down a certain path on purpose. The steps you're taking, the character you're developing, the intimacy with Him that you're cementing—these are more important than the specifics of getting to a certain destination. His main goal is not to confirm every single detail and demographic, all the fill-in-the-blank information that gives you absolute assurance to report to others about what you're doing next. Sometimes He just gives you enough for the one step that's directly in front of you so you'll learn to keep consulting Him and depending on Him all along the way. Later, as you look back through the lens of hindsight, you'll see that each of those steps, each disruption and apparent deviation from the target, each moment when you prayed more and sought His guidance more—this was actually His goal for you all along.

This is His will: you and Him, deepening in relationship, with each step of your journey laying a firm foundation for the next one as you honor Him every part of the way.

God's will for your life is found in hourly
increments of obedience.
Stop looking for God's will and just start living it.

Oh, how I wish my younger self had known this. I needed to *stop looking for God's will and just start living it.* My intentions were pure, but my focus was misplaced. Only in hindsight now do I see just how much needless worry and wasted energy I pumped into wanting *answers*—GIVE ME ANSWERS!—instead of simply surrendering fully into the tasks that were sitting right there in front of me. The burden I felt for being certain that I was in God's will, pursuing God's will, knowing God's will . . . all

He really wanted me to do was what I *already knew* to be true from His Word, no matter what my current situation. Then I would *be* in His will.

If I'd only done each task in excellence and for His glory . . . if I'd simply remained prayerful, depending on Him for my strength and peace . . . if I'd shown the love of Jesus to the people I met in these various phases of life . . .

This *was* His will.

Not out *there* in the future somewhere; right *here* in the tasks spread out before me.

Each new step was merely the next one in a long line of trusting steps He'd been leading me to take the whole time, working His purposes and plan in my life. All I needed to be focused on was being committed to honoring Him in every season—seeking *Him* instead of His will—and I would've enjoyed the journey a whole lot more. For good reason. I wouldn't have wasted time looking for the very thing I was already standing in the middle of.

I realize now that when I asked God to show me His will for my life, I was wanting Him to show me what the next twenty years would hold. But His will for me was to honor Him with what the next twenty *minutes* held.

And the next twenty minutes after that.

And the twenty minutes after that.

Instead of asking, "What is God's will for my life?" I want to encourage you to ask questions like these:

- What tasks and responsibilities are in front of me today?
- Am I doing them, or am I avoiding them?
- How can I honor God with my actions and attitudes right now?
- Am I obeying Him while I wait?

Honoring God with your *today*—by engaging in what He's set before you, by reacting to the unexpected without compromise, by choosing to walk in obedience to His Spirit, and by engaging fully with an attitude of gratitude—this *is* His will for your life. When you devote yourself to what He's given you to do today, instead of succumbing to fear and anxiety about your current circumstances and future, you'll continue to run smack-dab into God's will for you in each season. And even more, it's how you stay poised, positioned, and prepared for what's coming next.

I could never have imagined that the contentment and discipline I learned when I was single would give me the inner fortitude needed to stay committed in my twenty years (so far) of marriage.

I couldn't have known that the relationships and connections I made during my time in radio would make up the foundations of my ministry decades later.

I would never have guessed that the time I spent working in television—which fostered a lot of insecurity because I could never seem to find my place—gave me experience in front of cameras, which is exactly what I'd need for recording video-driven Bible study series years later.

I had no way of knowing that those years as a corporate trainer were actually honing the skill of standing in front of an audience and communicating a message clearly—which is the crux of what I do today when I teach God's words to thousands of women at a time.

How could I have guessed that the notes I took while preparing for those ten college-aged women would be some of the same notes that inspired whole chapters in future books I'd author or in teachings I'd deliver?

And I didn't realize that the discipline I learned when prioritizing my young family above all other opportunities would teach me to be unflinching in putting first things first through the next two decades.

It all mattered.

Every part of it.

The heroes you read about in the Bible—Ruth, Esther, Joseph, Mary—often they were ordinary young men and women, not superheroes. Just because their names and stories appear in Scripture doesn't make them any more special than you. They were faced with challenges that most of us know from our Bible storybooks. But in *their* lives, in *their* world, these now-famous moments were simply the circumstances and decisions facing them *that day.* God's will wasn't a mysterious riddle waiting to be answered somewhere in their future. God's will was in their faces. God's will was in their now. And the same thing is true for you.

Today is your mission. Today is your answer.

In God's timing, today holds the key to where He's taking you tomorrow.

15

NOTHING BY ACCIDENT

Do you ever wish you were somewhere else? Doing something different? Around different people? Living out different circumstances? Do you feel as though you shouldn't have to put up with some of the conditions you're forced to deal with? Why this? Why now? Why are you even here?

Know the feeling?

I'd like to introduce you to a young girl from the Bible. You may not know much about her story. In fact, we aren't even given her name. She was a servant in the home of a man named Naaman, who was a successful military commander for the Syrians, a nation who was at war with Israel. Despite his achievements, Naaman had a big problem. He had leprosy—a horrible, incurable, infectious disease that made life miserable for anyone who had it. In 2 Kings 5, Naaman went to the prophet Elisha to seek healing, and Elisha told him to go dip himself in the Jordan River seven times and his leprosy would be gone.

"What?!" Naaman said (and I'm paraphrasing here)—"I'm not getting into that nasty water. We've got nice clean rivers where I live. I'll go wash myself in one of those. Forget you!" But one of his servants came to him and said, "[Sir . . .] if the prophet had told you to do some great thing, would you not have done it? How much more should you do it when he only tells you, 'Wash and be clean'?" (2 Kings 5:13). *Okay, okay.* Naaman relented. He swallowed his enormous pride, held his nose, and went through with the Jordan River thing. His leprosy, miraculously, was healed.

But rewind a little bit, and you'll find that this unnamed servant girl was a major player in Naaman's noteworthy biblical drama. A native of Israel, she'd been taken captive during a Syrian raid on her homeland. Ripped from her family, torn from everything she'd ever known and loved, she was forced into slavery and ended up in the service of an army captain's wife. *Naaman's* wife.

This young woman was about as far away from her hopes and dreams as a person could possibly be—apparently abandoned by the God who'd advertised Himself as her protector and defender and refuge and deliverer.

And yet despite her circumstances, she was alert and engaged enough to care about her master's disease. Despite everything that had happened to her, she remained confident in the power of her God and believed that He could help Naaman. She didn't allow her distaste for her place in life to keep her from pointing someone to the Lord. One day, while speaking with Naaman's wife about his dreadful leprosy, she said, "If only my master were with the prophet who is in Samaria, he would cure him of his skin disease" (2 Kings 5:3).

Which, as you know, is exactly what happened.

Naaman may never have sought out Elisha if not for this young girl—a girl whose circumstances were not what she would've preferred. Instead, God's miraculous work was sparked into action by this little captive girl, seemingly at the wrong place at the wrong time, but apparently in God's place on God's time. Right where He wanted her to be. Right where He could use her to be a light for Him the most.

You've been uniquely made with design, with intention, and with meaning. God fashioned you just as you are, to display His glorious light through the wonder of His creation of you. But deliberately choosing how He wanted to make you—the *who* and *what* of you—is only part of your story. He also decided the *when* and the *where*. He chose both the timing of your life as well as the geography of your life.

Not only are *you* not an accident, but even the specifics of where you were born and the generation you've been born into are not accidents either. Your heavenly Father *meant* for you to be here—in this family dynamic, in this city or town, inside your own ethnic background, at this moment in history—even if unexpected circumstances have set you in a situation that you never imagined and do not prefer. Nothing has taken Him by surprise. And, surprise of all surprises, God can and will use it all—the good, the bad, and the ugly—to put you in the right place for His purposes to be accomplished through your life.

Just ask Naaman's servant girl.

Or Joseph, stuck in a foreign jail for something he didn't do (Genesis 39:19-23).

Or Ruth, widowed at a young age, having no real prospects for a fulfilling future (Ruth 1:11-17).

Or Esther, faced with death if she did what was right (Esther 4:10-14).

Or Mary, probably only a teenager when she found out she would give birth to the Savior of the world (Luke 1:31).

I could go on.

Each of these individuals was in a place he or she didn't

expect or likely desire to be. And maybe you are too. Maybe you've missed out on an opportunity to get into a certain school or sports league or club you wanted. Instead you're having to settle for plan B or C. And that's not where you want to be.

Maybe you've been through a recent breakup that broke your heart. You didn't see it coming. And you're having a hard time getting over it. There's no boyfriend in your Instagram profile pic, and that's just not where you intended to be.

Or maybe it's a position much more serious than that. Maybe you've endured a truly heavy load of loss or pain or abuse or abandonment in your short lifetime. And you've wished for a different kind of life more times than you can remember. Please hear me: *I'm so terribly sorry.* I really am. No one deserves to be mistreated. Nothing ever justifies injustice. Ever.

In situations like these, understanding and accepting the spiritual reality of God's allowing your *when* and *where* can be hard to digest. I've not been able to understand all the things that God has allowed into my own life, either, or the lives of people I love. It's often unthinkable that He would permit some of these events to take place. Being able to understand it requires an eternal perspective and vantage point that we simply don't have.

But here's what you do have: a certainty and confidence that "my times are in your hands" (Psalm 31:15 NIV). God loves you. He is good. And He intends only goodness for you. Your current circumstances do not mean that He has cruelly doomed you to heartache, unhappiness, and emotional distress. Instead, He alone is able to turn even these unexpected things, even evil things, into miraculous things. Somehow, He weaves them into the fabric of your life until they become threads of grace and glory, remnants of His power and grace. Then masterfully

He shines His light through these deeper, darker prisms of your window and reflects something beautiful.

Listen to me: nothing is so miserable that God cannot, over time, reframe your hard places into something valuable and positive, something redemptive and empowering. And when He does—if you'll let Him—you'll realize how everything that's happened to you actually put you in prime position for Him to do some amazing work in your life—things that wouldn't have happened unless you'd been through them, unless you'd been right there, right then. You'll find peace in believing that God's power, God's light, enables you to shine no matter what's been done to you, no matter where you are . . . because you are here, *right here*, on purpose. No accident. No way.

The apostle Paul put it this way . . .

> *He has made every nationality . . . and has determined their appointed times and the boundaries of where they live.* (ACTS 17:26)

God determined "appointed times." God chose "the boundaries" that whole groups of people would live in. He made "every nationality" for His own particular purpose. We exist *where* we are, *when* we are, for a reason, a *good* reason known only to Him, even if the reason may not seem good to us right now as we try to muscle through it.

He has uniquely designed you for this time and place.

Every era intersects with its own set of challenges and opportunities. It deals with its own questions. It reacts to its own national and world events. It faces its own areas where change is needed, where people are hurting, where confusion reigns, where spiritual lostness and hunger cause them to look for something they've not found before. And you've been placed here, right in the middle of these cultural dynamics. The Lord has chosen you—with all the uniqueness of your gifting, personality, and spiritual sensitivities—to live out your mission at your pinpoint on the globe, in your neighborhood and in your school. It is God's purpose and design that you are you, at this precise downbeat of time, ready and equipped for what He wants His people doing in this hour.

Nothing about you is ever an accident.

Any old place, any old time, wasn't how God envisioned you when He decided to create you and insert you into the life you are living. You're like the prophet Jeremiah, who was "only a youth" (Jeremiah 1:6) when God called him to be one of His voices to the people, leading up to and through some of their hardest days in history. At his age and station in life, Jeremiah felt ill-equipped for that kind of assignment. And yet God said to him . . .

> *"I chose you before I formed you in the womb.*
> *I set you apart before you were born. I appointed*
> *you a prophet to the nations."* (JEREMIAH 1:5)

He put Jeremiah *there,* in that location. He put him there *then*, in that generation. He not only made him *who* and *what* he was, but He uniquely created him and specifically ordained him to be His instrument in that particular time and place. Incredible, isn't it? That God would be so personal and intentional with us?

You are not an accident of chance. You are here for a God-purpose and a divine mission—to stand in His light and to use what He's specifically given you as a way of influencing and impacting the sphere around you.

This generation and your geographical location have been entrusted to you.

On purpose.

What are you going to do about it?

The fact that God is intentional about how He's hung the universe and how He's ordered your placement inside of it reflects His *sovereignty.* Remember that word. It means everything that happens to you; He either orders it or allows it. In His superior wisdom and knowledge, He makes decisions based on information from His unique position as God. Just because it may not make perfect sense from our finite perspective doesn't mean He cannot already see how He's working it together for your good and His glory.

Still, He cares deeply about how you feel while you're going through it, and He sympathizes with you because you're His girl. And yet recognizing His sovereignty means that you can rest easy knowing He is never surprised or shocked or taken off guard even when you are. Beyond that, it means that because of His foreknowledge, He has already prepared to act on your behalf in the middle of it. It means you're not alone. He's got your back.

So let me be clear. When bad things happen (and they will), He will weave it into the story of His greatness and ensure that its generational, eternal impact is something you could never have imagined in real time.

It's why that little servant girl, although in the "wrong place" at the "wrong time," could find herself in the ironically ideal spot for exalting her God in a strange land and drawing someone else to do the same. And it's why you—right here, right now— can be fully engaged in the complexity of your situation and live with a holy expectation that you're in the middle of a plan, a mission, an assignment that He planned specifically for you.

Every place is the perfect place for you to reflect His light.

That little girl with no name in the Bible could not have known the significance of her capture in the grand design of God's sovereign agenda. And neither can you. So today, if your current circumstances are not what you ever imagined they'd be—if your dreams have been dashed and your expectations unmet—if you've been taken captive by a life you don't prefer—if unexpected circumstances have kidnapped you into an unfamiliar reality you'd rather escape—and if you can't understand how any of this could ever be useful—remember, God has a sovereign plan, and He can make something beautiful from your life.

This is what He does.

If you'll trust Him where you are, and ask Him to open your eyes to what's happening around you, you may just find that *this place* is actually *the place* that's right in the center of His will for your life.

16

LIGHT AT THE END
OF THE TUNNEL

Kaleidoscopes are cool to look through, any way you turn them. You can even make one of your own. A homemade kaleidoscope is basically just a cardboard or plastic cylinder (think paper towel roll) with mirrors or some kind of reflective material—like foil or an old CD—placed inside at opposing angles from one another. By attaching a clear container of various objects to one end of the tube and *holding it up to the light*—this is key!—you can look through the other end and see a fascinatingly beautiful, changeable, multidimensional image.

But here's the thing. It doesn't really matter what you toss into that little container at the end. By the time it catches the light and is reflected back to your eye, it still comes out looking magnificent. You could put little colored beads or sequins or confetti sprinkles in there. You could make it with tiny seashells or bird feathers or flower petals. You could even fill the packet with gravel from the sidewalk, bits of hardware pieces from the garage, or shards of broken glass from the dustpan. The kaleidoscope doesn't care. Even the most unlikely, seemingly incompatible kind of stuff can be transformed into an orderly, symmetrical, strikingly gorgeous array of images.

Kaleidoscopes are just another version of a stained glass window—a metaphor for what God created your life to be and do when His light is illuminated through it. Without expensive gemstones or anything else particularly exquisite or expected, a kaleidoscope still emits a polished-looking product on the other end. It's all evidence again that *"His* light / *your* life" is always an incredible thing to see. This is, in fact, what *kaleidoscope* means—"beautiful to see." And you, my darling, are beautiful to see. Even if you have a hard time imagining certain bits and pieces of *who you are* being able to fit too "beautifully" into the picture your life sends out, you simply need to try seeing yourself in a different light.

In His light.

One of those difficult bits for me, when I was a teenager, was my mouth.

I talked too much. W-A-A-A-Y too much.

Talked too loud. Talked out of turn. Talked without thinking. Talked with the wrong tone of voice. I guess I just talked to hear myself talk. If there was any reason to open my mouth and say something, I took it. Never met a pause I couldn't drive a paragraph through.

So as you can imagine, people often told me—especially teachers and such who were trying to have class without interruption—"Priscilla. *Stop.* TALKING!" I actually heard words like those a lot.

- Be quiet! I mean it! NOW! You hear me?
- That's enough from you, Priscilla.
- Not another word, young lady.

Did I deserve it? Yes. Usually. Yes.

But I began to think of "talking" as *BAD*. I began to think that talking, in and of itself, was a problem. Talking got you into trouble. Talking, even though it could make people laugh (and I *loved* that part—still do), could also make them cry, or make them mad, or make them cut you a dirty look and decide to pull away from you. Unrestrained, immature talking could result in things you didn't want, like a trip to the office, or a call to your parents, or a friend with hurt feelings.

Most young women, when they have a problem like that, see only the problem. And the people around them usually see it as nothing but a problem too. They all see the problem as something to get rid of. It's something to stuff down and stop doing. It's bad. You're BAD.

My solution then? *Be quiet,* like everybody was telling me. *Shut up, Priscilla!* I did my best to choke back my words, to stifle my opinions, to stop communicating, even though the silence felt sticky, like it was unnaturally holding me back. I didn't feel free or fully myself. In fact, I felt like somebody else entirely, like somebody who wasn't me.

My parents could see that my swing to the opposite extreme wasn't healthy. I mean, they knew, of course, that I needed discipline. They didn't approve of those times when I wasn't considerate of others, when I was disobedient at school, when I was rude or disrespectful. They wisely knew when to give me consequences for the trouble I caused myself by my lack of self-control with my mouth.

But they also did something else. Something that I'm eternally grateful for.

They held it up to the light.

One day, they sat me down and asked me to consider the possibility that my ability and desire to communicate were maybe not the real problem. Maybe they were an opportunity.

If I would surrender my unrestrained and immature tongue to the Lord, I might just find that it was part of my God-given uniqueness He could use for His glory. If I would intentionally let Him control my tongue, then maybe—just maybe—He would make something good come from the way He'd uniquely created me.

For the first time, I saw the possibility that this "problem" was actually a pool of potential.

I want you to do the same thing. Dare to imagine that your quirks or interests or unique characteristics that make life a bit hard are not negatives at their core. Sure, if left unchecked, without the guidance of God's Spirit, they may lead you into sin, but that doesn't make them bad. Your passion or creative freedom or internal curiosity doesn't need to be thrown out. It just needs to be held up to the light. *His* light.

As I matured, I began to learn how to surrender my tongue to Him . . . as in, pausing before speaking. Asking Him to monitor my words. Checking inwardly first to see if I detected a ping of conviction over what I was about to say. My need for doing this isn't something I've outgrown. I still have to keep close tabs on my mouth, even today. I know I'll never be perfect at it. But by God's Spirit, I'm learning more and more how to guard my tongue.

Along the way, God did something amazing. He started using my voice as a microphone for His glory. People started inviting me to talk—and talk and talk and talk—about *Him*. And I'll tell you what, I still do it every chance I get. It's part of what led me to write the book that you're holding in your hands right now. God took a weakness of mine, and through my parents' understanding and His own shaping, the Holy Spirit renewed my mind, molded my character, and matured my self-control. He now continues inviting me to yield myself to Him, and He helps me live out the uniqueness of my identity through what once seemed like nothing but a severe struggle.

My weakness, in other words, was part of the clunky stuff that God deliberately chose to put into my kaleidoscope to demonstrate His strength. His light shining through something that once got other people's attention for all the wrong reasons now gets their attention a lot more often for much better reasons—reasons that line up with the mission I was put on this earth for.

What about you? What bits and pieces of your life don't look like they could ever fit anywhere into God's plan? What quirks or propensities seem more like liabilities than assets? Where do people get the most frustrated with you? Where do you get the most frustrated with yourself? What's your own story that goes along with my "talking" story?

Instead of remaining a sore subject that keeps taking you down, let the radiance of God's light fire it to life like a diamond inside your kaleidoscope, inviting others who share the same idiosyncrasies to come see for themselves how God can transform these dull spots into pockets of grace-infused radiance.

The kaleidoscope effect changes everything. On days when you're really battling, hoist your struggle up to the light and take a glimpse at what you're becoming.

It's not junk in there. Looks more like jewels.

All because there's light at the end of the tunnel.

TO THINK ABOUT

- What are the tasks stretched out before you in the next twenty-four hours? Take time to consider how your faithfulness to these things—no matter how boring—is part of your divine assignment.
- What are some of the unique things happening in the world right now that you find interesting or have compassion toward? Ask God to show you how He has uniquely equipped you to impact that area of society.
- In what area of your life do you experience a consistent struggle? How could this tendency be used by God to bring Him glory and lift up others? What would it look like for you to give that part of your life to Him daily?

TO TAKE AWAY

God's will is not a destination, waiting to be discovered. God's will is a present reality, an ongoing journey. To find it and live inside it, you simply need to be fully engaged in each "right now" moment of your life. Honor Him in the tasks that are before you.

Trust God's sovereignty. This means you can rest easy knowing He is never surprised or shocked or taken off guard even when you are. He has already prepared to act on your behalf. You're not alone. He's got your back. He will weave your circumstances into a beautiful testimony.

Your mission in life is not so much confined to a job description or a field of study. It's not a title or a role. Your mission is to serve God in your generation—in all your work, in all your roles, in each season of life.

EPILOGUE:
I'VE GOT YOU

I stood in the hospital corridor in stunned disbelief, my heart shattered in a million pieces as I looked into the tear-streaked faces of four beautiful young sisters. Alena, at fourteen, was the oldest, along with twelve-year-old Kaity and ten-year-old twins Olivia and Camryn.

This was the night that their mother, Wynter Danielle Pitts, had just been pronounced dead.

Technically these sweet girls are my second cousins. But they'd called me Auntie Silla from the first day they could utter enough words to call me anything at all. They felt more like nieces to me than distant relatives. We're family.

Many other members of our family swarmed the hospital as news spread of Wynter's passing. We all held each other that night—held Wynter's husband, held their girls, held the rest of our extended family—crying, praying, and singing praise songs around her cooling body. I cuddled the twins in my lap, rubbing their backs and wiping their tears with hands already wet from my own.

Around midnight, as the reality of loss set in, I was leaning back against the wall in that same stark hallway, standing just opposite Alena, who was being cradled in the warm embrace of another aunt—my sister, Chrystal. Watching them wordlessly for a moment, I savored the sight of this mature life touching and covering the younger one. It was beautiful enough to make me almost smile just a bit.

My eyes then shifted farther down the hall, where I noticed that for a few moments the hallway had cleared of everyone other than the women in our family. One was texting. Another had her face buried in her hands. Two of them were whispering to each other in mournful tones, while others just stared blankly ahead. All of us were there—aunts, sisters, sisters-in-law, a grandmother, cousins—individual women, unified in presence. I saw *us,* and I saw *her*—Alena, a motherless, teenage girl.

Stepping across the hallway, I tapped her on the shoulder. "Alena, look . . ." I said, pointing down the corridor to show her what I was seeing, this cocoon of feminine fortitude surrounding her.

"Do you see us, sweet girl?"

She nodded weakly.

Cupping her face in my hands, I whispered, "We've got you, little one. We've. Got. You."

She gave me a feeble smile. She understood. And so did I. Her aunties would be stepping up and stepping in to mother her and her little sisters through this tender phase of life, holding their hands and guiding them into adult womanhood, reminding them who they are and who they're becoming, filling in the missing pieces of the feminine puzzle that they'd be needing to decode without their mother's love and counsel.

It's with this same sentiment of love and desire that I've penned the pages of this book. Here I am, looking down the corridor at you, dear little sister. And I want you to know . . .

I see you.

I've taken this time with you seriously because I respect the fact that your life, despite being younger than mine, is not junior in size or in relative complexity. I consider you a full-fledged member of our sisterhood. You're in a *good* place at your age, with so much promise and possibility surrounding you and in front of you. But I know in many ways, if you're like most of us, you're also in some *hard* places. And I feel responsibility for giving you the kind of advice and perspective that'll match the intensity of what you're up against every day.

Finding your way into womanhood is filled with pitfalls that we all need help maneuvering around . . .

- When you feel discouraged. Outperformed. Insecure. Inferior.
- When you've been excluded and ignored. Overlooked and underappreciated.
- When you question your beauty—your body, your feelings, your personality.
- When your weaknesses and failings, your mistakes and missteps, make you feel unqualified to serve a big God.
- When you feel exhausted and worn out from driving to achieve and impress.
- When you're crippled by perfectionism and trying to live up to unattainable standards.
- When you've been constantly competing and comparing, sizing yourself up against every other girl or young woman you meet.
- When life happens and you're struggling—I mean, *seriously* struggling—against the strain, disappointment, and discouragement.

At these times and many others, you need some support and wisdom, some encouragement and reinforcement from other women who are determined to have your back.

So, hear me again . . . *I've got you.*

Maybe, like me, you've been surrounded by women all your life who've *had you.* I hope so. Maybe one of those women even gave you this book to read. In that case, it's been my honor to stand with her in supporting and encouraging you, no matter what you're facing today.

But if somehow the ball of mentorship has been dropped for you—if no one's seemed to care enough or has paid attention enough or loved enough or been present enough to tell you, it's been my privilege to share these things with you—not because I'm perfect, but just because I've been around a while and have learned a little. Wobbles, falters, missteps, and mercy will teach a girl a thing or two.

Or four . . . like the four big parts of this book you've just finished and that I hope you'll never, ever forget . . .

1. You are divinely designed. Handcrafted in God's image. Inside and out. A radiant expression of His creative genius and a reflection of His power and glory.
2. God's Spirit lives in you. Through faith in His cross, you are fully forgiven, fully free, fully alive.
3. You are not your struggle. You are not your behavior. You are not your feelings. You are not your experiences. Your identity is rooted in your new nature in Christ. You can now take back your peace, joy, and contentment. They are yours to keep.
4. You are on assignment, on mission, purposely placed in this generation by God's Spirit, to do not only big future things, but also the simple, faithful everyday things.

So, when tomorrow morning rolls around, here's what you need to remember:

Be **YOURSELF**—*"remarkably and wondrously made."* (PSALM 139:14)

Be **BLESSED**—*"with every spiritual blessing in the heavens in Christ."* (EPHESIANS 1:3)

Be **ASSURED**—*"he who started a good work in you will carry it on to completion."* (PHILIPPIANS 1:6)

Be on **MISSION**—*"he who calls you is faithful; he will do it."* (1 THESSALONIANS 5:24)

And as always, be **RADIANT.**

I am just one of a whole host of women who are cheering for you, praying for you, and celebrating God's work through you. Your generation will never be alone because a holy sisterhood will always have your back. We see you. We know who you are. So keep going without looking behind you. Keep pressing on without fear. Keep honoring God with a passion.

And remember . . . we've got you.

One generation will declare your works to the next and will proclaim your mighty acts. (PSALM 145:4)

ABOUT THE AUTHOR

A *New York Times* bestselling author, speaker, and actress, **Priscilla Shirer** is passionate about sharing God's Word with women of all ages, both the young and the young at heart. Put a Bible in her hand and a message in her heart, and you'll see why thousands meet God in powerful, personal ways through her words.

For the past twenty years, Priscilla has been in full-time ministry to women, speaking internationally and authoring more than two dozen books and Bible studies. She and her husband, Jerry, founded Going Beyond Ministries and count it as their privilege to serve believers across the entire spectrum of the body of Christ. Between writing and studying, she spends her days cleaning up after (and trying to satisfy the appetites of) three rapidly growing sons—Jackson, Jerry Jr., and Jude.